# Georgian London

## G E Mingay

*'Oh, London is a fine town*
*A very famous city,*
*Where all the streets are paved with gold*
*And all the maidens pretty.'*

George Colman
*Heir-at-Law*

B T BATSFORD Ltd,
London & Sydney

# Contents

First published 1975
© G E Mingay 1975
ISBN 0 7134 3045 1

Filmset by Servis Filmsetting Ltd, Manchester
Printed by The Anchor Press, Tiptree, Essex
for the publishers B T Batsford Ltd
4 Fitzhardinge Street London W1H 0AH
23 Cross Street Brookvale NSW 2100 Australia
Distributed in the United States by Hippocrene Books

# Preface

Anyone who writes today on Georgian London must begin with the two recent works which cover this period in the *History of London* series edited by Francis Sheppard: George Rudé's brilliant *Hanoverian London 1714–1808,* and the equally fine volume by Francis Sheppard, *London 1808–1870: the Infernal Wen.* The pioneer work of these two authors in gathering together the many scattered materials relating to London has greatly eased the task of other writers, and I am one who is greatly indebted to them.

The Select Bibliography at the end of this volume notes these and a number of other works which I have found valuable, although the bibliography does not pretend to be in any way a comprehensive list of the vast literature which has grown up around our capital city.

# Acknowledgment

The author and publishers wish to thank the following for their kind permission to reproduce copyright illustrations: the London Museum for the front endpaper, and for pages 21, 22, 31, 33, 35, 48–9, 73 (*top*), 88 (*bottom*), 126–7; the Victoria & Albert Museum for both illustrations on the title page, and for pages 8–9, 56–7, 66, 71, 76–7 (*bottom*), 81, 86–7, 89, 129; the Greater London Council for page 23; the National Portrait Gallery for page 62; the Mansell Collection for pages 69, 76–7 (*top*), 106, 116, 122–3, 135, 156–7; the Dowager Lady Hillingdon for page 83; the National Maritime Museum for page 88 (*top*); the British Museum for pages 75, 82, 95, 114–5, 158; the Radio Times Hulton Picture Library for pages 148–9 (*bottom*); Mary Evans Picture Library for pages 152–3 (*top*). The other illustrations appearing in the book are the property of the publishers, who would like to extend their thanks to Douglas Sellick for the picture research.

*Right* Pickpockets at work at St Bartholomew's Fair, 1739.

*Overleaf* The Strand, by Thomas Malton, 1796.

# The Expanding Metropolis

'I think the full tide of human existence is at Charing Cross.'

Dr Johnson

At the opening of the Georgian era London stood, as it had done for centuries, at the centre of English life. The sway of its influence derived not merely from its position as the capital city and centre of government: it was also the country's greatest mart for commerce and finance, the hub of overseas trade, a major centre of manufacturing and the home of many highly-skilled craftsmen. London housed, too, the most important courts of law, and provided the major centres for the developing professions of the law, medicine, architecture and civil engineering. The capital's famous sights, its theatres, fashions, shops and amusements drew in visitors like a magnet. Some came regularly every winter, as did the aristocracy from their country estates; others, less well-heeled, came only occasionally as opportunity offered, or perhaps as the one really great experience of a lifetime. More sinisterly, the combination of the wealthy and the unwary attracted also a large criminal class of footpads, robbers, pickpockets, tricksters and hucksters who made their own distinctive contribution to the excitement of congested city streets. All these varied aspects of Georgian London must find some place in these pages.

To William Cobbett, writing in the closing years of the period, London was the 'great wen', an enormous expanding sponge that absorbed fields and villages, and attracted its stockjobbers, fundholders and tax-eaters from 50 miles away. John Byng, like Cobbett a traveller who yearned for the peace and beauty of the countryside, agreed with him in detesting London's bustle, smoke and manners. 'A long London winter bends me to earth', he remarked:

> My nerves are terribly weak, and my chest is alarmingly sore;
> I feel in London like the enraged musician, stunn'd by noises,
> cries, and rape; and nearly driven over, every day, by curricles;
> and, if I mount my horse, can hardly escape from a Brentford
> stage: the ceaseless account of diversions and fashions make me
> sick; and I will not accord to the unnatural hours. Nerve-worn,
> and with reason, I must, tho' melancholy to go alone, take the
> field.

Byng was condemned to find his employment in the capital, but his pleasure was found in touring the country in search of ruins and other remnants of antiquity:

> I leave town, every year, with more pleasure, from being
> incapable (call it so) of tasting the *delights* of fashionable hours,
> and from ignorance of the fashionable tongue; hoping that,
> even yet, there must exist in the country, by the want of baneful
> intercourse, somewhat more purity, and civility; where you may
> escape eternal insult, and viewing the ill-treatment of every

animal who cannot resist: Besides, the uproar of a small
London house, with stairs like Jacob's Ladder, makes my blood
to boil . . .

For others London held perpetual fascination: the sheer size
of the city was itself an attraction, offering life in all its variety.
Dr Johnson remarked that 'when a man is tired of London, he
is tired of life: for there is in London all that life can afford'.
James Boswell commented to Dr Johnson on 'the cheerfulness
of Fleet Street', and the great man replied: 'Why, sir, Fleet
Street has a very animated appearance; but I think the full
tide of human existence is at Charing Cross.' In *The Spleen or
Islington Spa*, George Colman's characters comment on the
pros and cons of the town:

'The full tide of human existence' –
Charing Cross a little after the time of
Dr Johnson (1807).

*Mrs Rubrick*: It's impossible to keep in town all the summer, let the proverb go as it will, sister Tabby! – to be cooped up in the Row, amidst the smell of the printing-house, and Dolly's beef-steaks, all the Dog-days? – No, give me fresh air, and Islington! – All the world shut up their houses in London at this time of the year, and resort to the watering-places.

*Mrs Tabitha*: So much the worse, sister Rubrick! I have never resorted out of the sound of Bow-bell these fifty years – nor ever desired it – winter or summer, all's one to Tabitha! – And as to the watering-places, I'm told nobody goes there, that's fit to go anywhere else! – Cripples, and sharpers! phtisicky old gentlewomen, and frolicksome young ones! Married ladies that want children, unmarried ladies that want sweethearts, and gentlemen that want money! Newgate out of town, the London hospital in the country, sister!

And, as Horace Walpole argued, London offered more than the full tide of human existence: in the swarming capital one could find what was unobtainable in the country – anonymity:

Were I a physician, I would prescribe nothing but *recipe ccclxv drachm. Londin.* Would you know why I like London so much? Why, if the world must consist of so many fools as it does, I choose to take them in the gross, and not made into separate pills, as they are prepared in the country. Besides, there is no being alone but in a metropolis: the worst place in the world to find solitude is in the country: questions grow there, and that unpleasant Christian commodity, neighbours. Oh! they are all good Samaritans, and do so pour balms and nostrums upon one, if one has but the toothache, or a journey to take, that they break one's head. (1743)

The population of London grew rapidly in the Georgian age. It was by far the largest city in England, and already the largest in Europe. During the Stuart era, the number of London's inhabitants had increased enormously: the capital's population doubled in the first half of the seventeenth century to reach a total of some 400,000. Subsequently the pace of growth seems to have slackened, but the city held well over half a million people at the beginning of the eighteenth century, and some 675,000 by 1750 – and this at a time when the national rate of population growth across the whole country was almost certainly very slow. When the first official census was taken in 1801 it showed London to have a population of 900,000; at the third census, twenty years later, the capital was well on the way towards its second million with a total of 1,379,000 – equivalent to a tenth of the whole population of England and Wales.

London's dominant position as a population centre is

perhaps best shown by some comparisons. London and Paris were by far the greatest cities in Europe, but although the total population of France in the first half of the eighteenth century was about four times that of England, London had passed Paris's total well before the end of the seventeenth century. By the end of the eighteenth century the number of London's citizens was over 60 per cent greater than the 550,000 of the French capital. In 1750 only about $2\frac{1}{2}$ per cent of France's population lived in Paris; London, at the same time, housed about 11 per cent of England's population. In the provinces of England the eighteenth century saw a rapid growth of major ports and centres of industry. In the first half of the century Bristol doubled its population from 48,000 to 100,000; Liverpool rose from 6,000 to 35,000; Norwich had 56,000 by 1750, while Manchester, Sheffield and Birmingham all had between 30,000 and 50,000 at that date. But in 1750 London's population was twice as great as all these put together. Unlike the older cities of Norwich and Bristol, the greatest days of Liverpool, Manchester, and Birmingham were still to come. Nevertheless, in 1821, London had over ten times as many people as any of these burgeoning creations of the industrial revolution.

Why London's pre-eminence? What were the dynamics of its expansion? The causes of growth were certainly not to be found in the natural increase of its native population: on balance, London was a consumer, not a spawner of humankind. In the first half of the eighteenth century the annual number of deaths was in excess, sometimes frighteningly in excess, of the number of baptisms. Gregory King, the famous statistician of the late seventeenth century, believed that London had a markedly lower proportion of children than the rest of the country. The reasons he gave 'why each marriage in London produces fewer children than the country marriages' included 'the more frequent fornications and adulteries; greater luxury and intemperance; a greater intensiveness of business; the unhealthfulness of the coal smoke; and a greater inequality of age between the husbands and wives.'

Whether or not he was right about this, London certainly experienced higher mortality among infants and young children than did the provinces. The adverse margin between deaths and baptisms was at its greatest between 1724 and 1742, some 30 years after King analyzed the problem. In the worst of these years burials exceeded baptisms by over 18,000 a year, and only one child in four survived to his fifth birthday. London, like all large centres of population in this period, was dangerously insanitary and disease-ridden, but the malady which seems to have accounted for much of the excessive mortality of the early Georgian age was man-made – gin. The gin orgy eventually passed away, but even in the later part of the eighteenth century the margin between baptisms and burials, though normally positive, was still too small to account for the great increase in London's population. The ready flow of migrants to the capital was evidently the major factor in its growth.

In the 1750s, it is estimated, London was gaining through migration a net increase of 8,000 souls a year. This, of course, was not a new development: London had always been a magnet for the footloose, the adventurous, the aspiring. Gregory King thought that 8 per cent of the capital's population was made up of 'sojourners', while servants accounted for another 13 per cent. Young people flocked in from provincial towns and the countryside to seek employment, perhaps as domestic servants, as apprentices in London's many and varied trades, or as labourers in the numerous occupations that depended on London's docks and trade. Irish labourers then, as now, supplied much of the stock of unskilled heavy labour, and were employed in building, portering, coal-heaving and petty hawking. There were also colonies of French, German, Dutch and Portuguese, many of them connected with overseas shipping and with business houses dealing with foreign transactions. Numbers of Huguenot weavers had brought their skills to London following the persecution of the French Protestants and the Revocation of the Edict of Nantes in 1685. There were bands of negroes and Indian lascar seamen, and more numerous, the Jews, many of them Polish or German, who may have totalled 20,000 by the end of the eighteenth century. The wealthier Jews, merchants and financiers, settled in the City or in the West End; the poorer concentrated in St James's and in Whitechapel, Houndsditch, Petticoat Lane and Mile End. Wordsworth, in 'The Prelude', noted these and many more:

> Now homeward through the thickening hubbub, where
> See, among less distinguishable shapes,
> The Italian, with his frame of Images
> Upon his head; with Basket at his waist
> The Jew; the stately and slow-moving Turk
> With freight of slippers piled beneath his arm.
> Briefly, we find, if tired of random sights
> And haply to that search our thoughts should turn,
> Among the crowd, conspicuous less or more,
> As we proceed, all specimens of Man

*Through all the colours which the sun bestows,*
*And every character of form and face,*
*The Swede, the Russian; from the genial South,*
*The Frenchman and the Spaniard; from remote*
*America, the Hunter-Indian; Moors,*
*Malays, Lascars, the Tartar and Chinese,*
*And Negro Ladies in white muslin gowns.*

For the migrants, the main attractions of London were the endless opportunities the capital offered for employment, for rising in the world, for society and entertainment, for crime – for becoming a part of the bustling, thriving, vibrant life of the metropolis, a life so excitingly different from the humdrum existence of the country town and village. London was England's great centre of commerce, the entrepot through which flowed the major part of the nation's exports and imports. Its own domestic market for food, drink, clothing, coal, and cheap manufactures was vast by the standards of the time. All the major produce markets were located there: Smithfield for livestock; Billingsgate for fish and coal; Covent Garden for fruit and vegetables; Mark Lane, Bear Quay and Queenhithe for grain; Haymarket, Smithfield, Whitechapel and the Borough for hay; Blackwell Hall for cloth; and Southwark and Leadenhall for leather and poultry. Merchants, shippers, tradesmen, and their clerks and assistants, thronged these expanding centres of trade, and they in turn employed an army of porters, carters, warehousemen, watchmen and messengers. Docks, shipyards, ships and lighters along the Thames created further demands for labour, both skilled and unskilled. Then there were the manufacturers, large and small, concerned with a variety of cloth-making, clothing, leather goods, beer, spirits, soap, glass, furniture and a host of other commodities. Branches of particular trades dominated certain districts of London: silk-weaving became identified with Spitalfields, for example, and clothing with Aldgate and Whitechapel. Many a migrant, however, directed his feet towards the City and found his first job in an inn or coffee house.

The presence in London for much of the year of the court, Parliament, the law courts, and the nobility and gentry up for 'the season', made the capital a centre for the 'conspicuous consumption' of the wealthy, in Professor Fisher's phrase. Luxury trades flourished, and their workshops and retail establishments offered many openings for the young man whose parents could afford to pay for his apprenticeship. The goldsmiths, silversmiths and jewellers, the carriage-makers, furnishers and booksellers, the vintners, and tea and coffee merchants, the perruque-makers, silk merchants and purveyors of high fashion were all sources of employment, and perhaps even the first step towards a fortune.

London's need for food had a considerable influence on eighteenth-century England, affecting not merely the home counties, but farming and trade at a very great distance from the capital. In his *Tour through England and Wales*, first published in 1724–26, Daniel Defoe commented again and again on the variety of ways in which agricultural production and provincial markets were geared to the demands of the London population. Bedfordshire and Hertfordshire both served as granaries for the capital, while the greatest provincial corn market was at Farnham, where, Defoe reported, on market days hundreds of teams drew loads of wheat to be sent to Guildford for grinding, and thence on by barge to London. Cattle, driven all the way from the Welsh mountains and the remote Scottish highlands, were fattened for London markets in the midlands and the southern counties, and in Norfolk between Norwich and Yarmouth. Sheep from Lincolnshire and Leicestershire were kept on the Essex marshes near Tilbury until prices rose in London near Christmas time. Cheese, bacon and malt were brought down the Thames in barges from Gloucestershire and Wiltshire for the satisfaction of London's housewives, together with Cheddar cheese from more distant Somerset, and Stilton – the 'English Parmesan' – from Huntingdonshire, eaten, said Defoe, with a spoon so as *not* to miss the 'mites or maggots' that swarmed thick round it.

Every August turkeys and geese were sent on their way to London from Norfolk and Suffolk, travelling in carts or on foot, often in droves a thousand or more strong. 'They have counted 300 droves of turkeys . . . pass in one season over Stratford Bridge on the River Stour, on the road from Ipswich to London', said Defoe, while many more travelled by way of Newmarket Heath, and by Sudbury and Clare. The poultry drives continued until the end of October, 'when the roads begin to be too stiff and deep for their broad feet and short legs to march in'. Epping butter was especially popular in the capital, but had to be supplemented by supplies from further afield, shipped from the east coast ports of Northumberland, Yorkshire, and Suffolk. Cheshire cheese came by sea all the way round Wales and Land's End and up the Channel to London. Fish came in from ports all round the east and south coasts, and the mackerel from Folkestone, and Whitstable oysters, were brought up the Thames by the Kentish hoys, together with grain and hops from Faversham, and fruit from the Medway valley.

Fruit and market-garden produce for Covent Garden came from nearby Lewisham, Plumstead or the Sandy district of Bedfordshire, and indeed from all the home counties. At a later period the growing of potatoes for the capital became very profitable. Some 50 years after Defoe's account, Arthur Young, in his *Southern Tour*, found potatoes were especially favoured as a crop because of 'the great price potatoes bear in the summer'. Some years later, in 1789, the Honourable John Byng (later fifth Viscount Torrington) remarked on the 'amazing price of straw' in London: it was dearer than hay, so he was told. 'What's the reason? Shall I tell you? It is because London is so overgrown, and so crowded by horses, that the consumption of straw is, within these few years, doubled; consequently, the adjacent counties, that are much under grass, cannot supply the metropolis, as formerly; straw then must be fetched from afar. This devilish increase of London will in time cause a famine, because it cannot be supplied.'

London required not only food and straw, but also coal for fuel and raw materials. The carriage of coal, timber, and other goods that came by sea to London employed a large proportion of the country's shipping resources. It is clear that as London grew and demanded more food, fuel and raw materials, as well as finished products not made in the capital, the effects on the country's economy as a whole must have been very considerable. In the first half of the century London was growing while the population of the rest of the country was stationary or even declining. The demand emanating from the capital must have had a marked impact on the progress of innovation in agriculture, industry and transport. Again, since a large proportion of the population had at least some brief acquaintance with the capital, its shops, businesses and social life, London exerted a steady pressure for change on provincial towns and villages, particularly those nearest the city. Not least of its influences was the taste for new commodities and fashions which visitors and migrants bore away with them – in things like tea, coffee, wines, cloth, dress and furniture.

Such was the volume of London's need for farm and other produce that the roads in the clayland districts near the capital were, as Defoe commented, 'perfectly frightful to travellers', and killed great numbers of horses 'by the excess of labour in these heavy ways'. The midland counties, he wrote, 'drive a very great trade with the city of London . . . by consequence, the carriage is exceeding great, and also that all the land carriage of the northern counties necessarily goes through these

counties, so the roads have been plowed so deep, and materials have been in some places so difficult to be had for repair of the roads that all the surveyors' rates have not been able to repair them . . .' The solution, as Defoe noted, was to establish turnpike trusts which, for 'an easy toll', repaired the highways, 'the benefit of a good road abundantly making amends for that little charge the travellers are put to at the turnpikes'.

Within the capital, too, there were inadequate roads and horrible congestion as the coaches, carts and wagons from the country competed for right of way with the 2,500 private carriages and the 1,100 carriages for hire which thronged the streets in 1739. Fortunately the Thames, and lesser streams like the Wey and the Lea, met much of London's transport needs; and after 1801 these were supplemented by the London link with the Grand Trunk Canal and the inland waterway system of the midlands. In the second half of the century new bridges at Westminster and Blackfriars, and new roads, came to the rescue of wheeled traffic, and by the early years of the nineteenth century as many as 50 turnpike trusts were established in the vicinity of the capital, while a number of the main thoroughfares, Oxford Street and Marylebone Road, for instance, were turnpiked. In 1790 John Byng could remember with affection the old roads and mode of travelling of his youth

Blackfriars Bridge under construction, 1765. New roads and bridges helped to ease London's traffic problems.

18

40 years earlier: how the road crossing Blackheath to Eltham 'became so narrow that a servant was always sent half a mile in advance, to remove obstructions'. He went on:

> I am just old enough to remember turnpike roads few, and those bad; and when travelling was slow, difficult, and, in carriages, somewhat dangerous: but I am of the very few, (perhaps alone,) who regret the times (I mean not living in them) when England afforded to the pleasure of the observant traveller, a variety of manners, dress and dialect. In former tours I have (gravely and wisely) remark'd upon the influx of vice pour'd in upon every corner of the country by the quick and easy communication of travel. In the days of bad roads, the country cou'd not be strip'd of its timber, or despoil'd of its honesty, cheapness, ancient customs, and civility: every gentleman, then, was bow'd to with reverence, and 'A good morning to you, master, Good evening, Good journey to you Sir', were always presented; with every old-fashion'd wish, and compliment of the season: now, every abuse, and trickery of London are ready to be play'd off upon you. (*Torrington Diaries*)

The growth of its population inevitably involved the physical expansion of the capital. Neighbouring fields and pleasure grounds were steadily eaten up, and former villages merged into a continuous urban sprawl in face of the insatiable demand for more houses, more warehouses, shops, yards, stables and factories. Horace Walpole was one contemporary who commented on this process:

A view of the Flask Tavern and garden at Chelsea, 1761. By the end of the eighteenth century, Chelsea had largely lost this rural character, and was becoming firmly welded to the metropolis.

> There will soon be one street from London to Brentford; ay, and from London to every village ten miles round! Lord Camden has just let ground at Kentish Town for building fourteen hundred houses – nor do I wonder; London is, I am certain, much fuller than ever I saw it. I have twice this spring been going to stop my coach in Piccadilly, to inquire what was the matter, thinking there was a mob – not at all; it was only passengers. Nor is there any complaint of depopulation from the country. (1791)

When George 1 came to the throne in 1714, London's built-up area stretched in the north as far as Spitalfields, and embraced Shoreditch and Bun Hill Fields, and was edging out, too, towards Islington, Sadler's Wells and Tottenham Court; on the west St Mary le Bon, New Bond Street, St James's Palace and Buckingham House (later Palace) represented the limits; southwards London had crept down to Tothill Fields and the Horse Ferry across the Thames, where Lambeth Bridge now stands, while probing fingers had already reached Vauxhall, Newington Butts and Bermondsey; eastwards Rotherhithe and Wapping, Cable Street, the Mile End Road and

Bethnal Green had succumbed to invasion by bricks and mortar; ribbon development had reached Hackney and Kentish Town, and Paddington and Bayswater were new suburbs, as were also Kensington, Hammersmith, Chelsea and Fulham. Wandsworth, Clapham, Camberwell and Peckham had now become familiar names to many Londoners, and riverside development had moved eastwards towards Limehouse and the Isle of Dogs on the north bank of the Thames, and to Deptford and Greenwich on the south bank.

As London expanded the contrast between the aristocratic, residential West End and the more plebeian, commercial and industrial East End took firmer shape. As James Boswell observed, 'one end of London is like a different country from the other in look and in manners'. The causes of this difference were obvious enough. The East End developed round the ancient business heart of the City, and in the vicinity of the docks, shipyards and produce markets which provided the inhabitants with so much of their employment. It was natural, too, that London's staple industries should grow up in and around this area, where fuel, raw materials and plenty of cheap labour were all to hand. The West End, by contrast, grew up in different and more rural surroundings, between the Houses of Parliament and the government buildings in Whitehall, the old palace and park of St James's, Hyde Park to the west, and the fields lying to the north of Piccadilly and beyond Oxford Street. This area lacked docks, warehouses, business offices and workshops, and the mode of its development prevented the intrusion of these unattractive appurtenances of commerce.

When Oxford Street ended in the fields: the turnpike at Tyburn showing the entrance to Oxford Street.

A New PLAN of the CITY of LONDON, WESTMINSTER, and SOUTHWARK

To the Right Honourable Sir GEORGE THOROLD Knight & Baronet, Lord Maior of the City of LONDON. This Plan is most Humbly Dedicated

Much of the land in the West End was in the hands of aristocratic and corporate owners, and the urban growth was carefully planned and controlled. Streets and squares were laid out for residential purposes under the terms of private local Acts, and the long leases under which the properties were held placed restrictions on non-residential uses, though in practice the restrictive covenants were not always easy to enforce.

In the East End growing areas like Stepney, Spitalfields, Wapping, St George in the East and Bethnal Green, were built up in a higgledy-piggledy fashion by individuals who often held the land by copyhold from lords of manors. They usually built on the basis of short leases (often for a period of 31 years), with little or no attempt to control the use of the premises. Houses, shops, workshops and warehouses were built cheek by jowl, without plan or system, the principal object being to cram in as many rent-producing buildings to the acre as possible. Certainly the London Building Act of 1774 laid down requirements for materials and the wall thicknesses of new buildings, but the object of the Act was to prevent fire and the creation of dangerous structures: there were no provisions for regulating the width of the streets or the setting of minimum

Cobbett's 'great wen' in embryo: London as it was very early in the Georgian era.

standards for light and ventilation. The short length of the leases, and the widespread practice of subletting, also made for indifference over providing amenities and maintenance. Repairs were neglected, and some buildings rapidly declined into insanitary slums, while others, despite the Building Act, became unsafe and were reported as 'ready to fall' – as sometimes, indeed, they did.

A view of London and the Thames from the Horse Ferry (Jan Griffier the Elder, c. 1710).

To the west and north of the City, the large London landowners were busily creating a different kind of environment. Already, in the later seventeenth century, the Bedford estate by Gray's Inn in Holborn had been transformed into a complex of new streets, such as Bedford Row and Theobald's Road, while further west the London squares had already made an appearance in the 1630s, with the Covent Garden Piazza and Leicester Fields (later Square). The later years of the seventeenth century saw the development of Bloomsbury Square – the first open space to be so called – and the further squares of Soho, Red Lion and St James's, as well as Lincoln's Inn Fields. The lavish use of space and the standard of building were influenced not merely by the desire to achieve a pleasantly open effect, but also by the fact that the landlord himself intended to make the square his London residence, as did the Earl of Southampton in Bloomsbury Square, and the Earl of St Albans in St James's.

In the Georgian era similar schemes were promoted by the Earl of Scarborough in Hanover Square, and there were also the Earl of Burlington's projects in the Piccadilly area, and developments in Cavendish, Grosvenor and Berkeley Squares. All these were completed or at least begun by the 1730s. A lull in building activity followed, influenced by the slow growth of the landowners' agricultural incomes and the wartime

Bloomsbury Square in 1787, showing the lavish use of space which marked the great landowners' development of the West End.

ifficulties of borrowing money. After the Seven Years' War 1756–63) construction schemes were again pushed forward – roducing Portland Place, Bedford, Portman and Manchester quares, George Dance's Finsbury Square, the Adam brothers' \delphi by Charing Cross, and Sir William Chambers's omerset House on the riverside near the Temple. In the 790s the Foundling Hospital estate, including a new square, 3runswick Square, was developed between the Bedford roperties to the west and Gray's Inn Road to the east.

It was Thomas Wriothesley, fourth Earl of Southampton, who introduced the principle which formed the basis of the reat spate of late seventeenth-century and subsequent Georgian square-building. Erecting his own mansion in the elds which became Bloomsbury Square, he let his first building eases in 1661. The plots were let at low ground rents to lessees who were required to build houses of a substantial character. eases were at first for periods of 42 years, but had advanced o a standard 99 years by the late eighteenth century; the ouses reverted to the landlord at the termination of the lease. he falling in of these leases, and their renewal at higher rents, vas an important factor in the growth of the incomes of great andowners in the late eighteenth and early nineteenth enturies. The Earl of Southampton also originated the idea of he square as the centre-piece of a residential unit comprising ts own lesser streets and shops, a 'little town' as it was called, vith a life and character of its own. 'The Bloomsbury unit', vrote Sir John Summerson, 'was organic from the start and emained one of the most charming and sought-after suburbs f London until, as part of the Bedford estate, it grew eastwards nd northwards and became lost in the criss-cross of the 3loomsbury of the later Georgians.'

23

Golden Square, a less aristocratic milieu than the great squares, but still a good example of the creation of permanent open spaces in the heart of Georgian London (1754).

The landowner was the aristocratic originator of the square and he laid down the general characteristics of the scheme, but the actual execution of the project depended on the collaboration of the speculative builders who built and sold the houses. These speculators might be financiers who acquired blocks of plots for re-sale but might also build the houses, or else small builders, in fact building craftsmen, who took a lease on a plot or two and built the houses themselves with the help of other craftsmen. The names of some leading speculators survive in the names of the streets they built – Sir Thomas Bond and Sir Thomas Clarges, Richard Frith (of Frith Street, Soho), Colonel Panton (of Panton Street), and Gregory King who gave his name to King Square. There was in addition the great Barbon, who was active all over London in the later years of the seventeenth century. Among other schemes, he was responsible for replacing the Tudor mansion of the Essex House estate, with its grounds set attractively on the riverside south of the Strand, by the mundane 'taverns, alehouses, cockshops and vaulting schools' of Essex Street. Even the personal intervention of Charles II could not prevent this. Evidently, to secure the protection of historic buildings from the predatory hands of the speculator was as difficult then as now.

Later builders of the first importance included James Burton, who was responsible for much of the development of the Foundling Hospital estate in Brunswick Square and Guildford Street in the 1790s. From this early success he went on to the Bedford, Skinners', Lucas, Regent's Park and Eyre estates. He is thought to have built houses worth a total of nearly two million pounds – an enormous sum in those days – and he also participated in Nash's famous Regent Street project. His son was Decimus Burton, the celebrated architect who, in Sir John Summerson's view, 'does not deserve to be so *very* much more famous than his extraordinary father'. Another great figure who followed in Burton's footsteps on the Bloomsbury scene was Thomas Cubitt. He was the first builder to eschew the system of subcontracting the work to specialist groups of craftsmen, and instead employed all the various tradesmen on a permanent wage basis. This system demanded a steady flow of projects to keep his men employed, and Cubitt became the greatest contractor of the late Georgian period. He was already well-known before undertaking the south side of Tavistock Square for the Duke of Bedford in 1821. He then helped to develop Woburn Place, Endsleigh Street and Gordon Square, subsequently taking on parts of Belgrave Square and much of Pimlico for the Grosvenor estate. By 1828 he was employing as many as a thousand men.

Much of the new building, however, even in the fashionable suburbs of the West End, was done by obscure small master-builders. Frequently the craftsman-builder was supervised by an architect and was required to work to drawings and specified materials, but very satisfactory houses might often be built without this control. Such builders required little capital, since the lease often provided for only a 'peppercorn' rent to be paid for the first year or two, by which time the builder expected to have completed the shell of the house and to have sold it. A system of barter and credit enabled him to engage the services of other craftsmen, and the completion of the interior was undertaken by the purchaser. It could be a highly profitable business, but also a risky one, and the small builders, mainly bricklayers and carpenters, who took on these projects featured frequently in the bankruptcy lists.

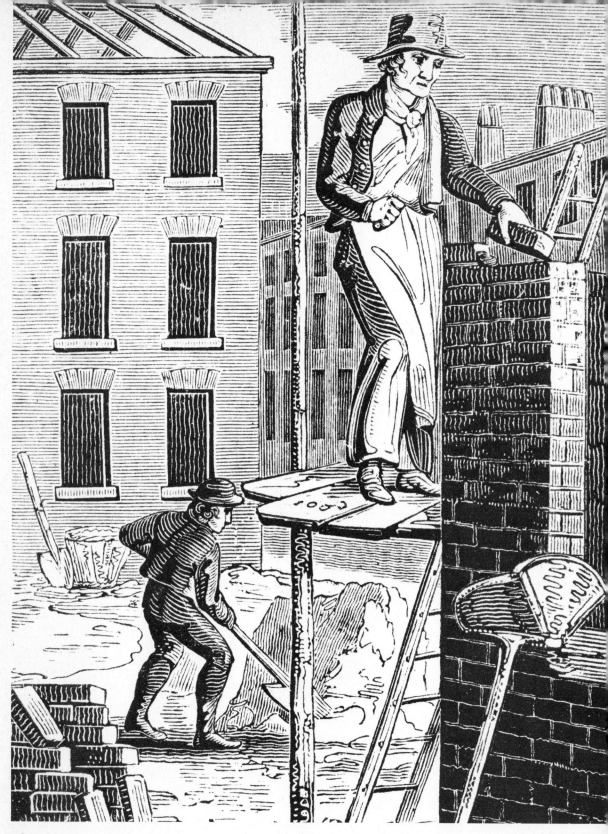

umbers (*above*) and bricklayers (*left*).
espite the activities of the great
ontractors such as James Burton and
homas Cubitt, many houses even in
e fashionable districts were erected
y independent master craftsmen such
 these.

The physical expansion of London required many thousands of building workers and gave rise to much employment in the production, importing and transport of building materials. The millions of bricks needed came mainly from the nearby brick-kilns using the London clay, but the more expensive types, such as the 'cutting bricks' used for window arches and decoration, were from further afield. The standard bricks used for outside walls were the 'grey' – usually yellowish-brown – stocks, good hard bricks which replaced the early red stocks as 'hot-coloured' bricks went out of fashion. The cheapest 'place' bricks, containing a high proportion of ash, were used for interior work, thus sowing the seeds of later structural problems. The timber employed was mainly Baltic fir, shipped from Danzig, Riga or Memel, but English oak, and occasionally mahogany from the West Indies, were used for the best structural work and joinery. Roof tiles were replaced by slates after 1765, when Lord Penrhyn began exporting slates from his quarries at Dolawen in north Wales. The glass used for glazing was of the crown variety, made in circular sheets without lead, much of it manufactured in Newcastle and shipped down the east coast in the colliers. Stone was little used for houses, as distinct from public buildings, and then only for porches, window dressings and cornices, although Purbeck stone was frequently used for paving the halls. It is remarkable that this loosely-regulated system of speculative building, which depended on architects who often had little or no formal training, and obscure craftsmen-builders, who naturally had an eye for economy in materials, should have resulted in houses so pleasing in their plain design, so attractive in their interior refinements of rococo ceilings and their exterior embellishments of wrought-iron work, and so substantial as to have survived the rigours of London's traffic and atmosphere for well over a century and more.

As analyzed by Steen Eiler Rasmussen the development of Georgian house styles in London might be called a form of '"hard" classicism'. While formerly the front of a house had been treated as a relief, made up of materials differing in colour and degree of hardness, 'now it was only regarded as a homogeneous block of brick and the joinery did not belong to the architecture itself. The walls alone constituted the architecture . . . Neither was the roof of any consequence from an architectural point of view; it was a mere technical necessity, architecturally just as indifferent as the chimney. It was preferable to disguise both with a parapet.'

The rich Englishman, Rasmussen remarks, continued to

27

accumulate riches, but he certainly did not spend them on th
exterior decoration of his house. And after the introduction o
the window tax, the area of the walls compared with that of th
windows increased. The contrast with the architecture of th
Continent shows fundamentally different views. On th
Continent architects worked to give the house an impressio
of heaviness, especially at the base. The English house did no
pretend to be heavy below and light at the top. It was a simple
plain shell of brick around the rooms, and its virtues lay in it
simplicity and the brilliantly economical use it made of th
typically narrow-fronted site. To obtain maximum advantag
of space the houses were built deep, with the entrance place
not in the middle but to one side of the front. Many houses o
this sort survive, those facing St James's Park and Hyde Park
for instance, and those in Queen Anne's Gate and Bloomsbury
Where the front was rather wider, as in the Bloomsbury square
the houses were made less deep, and a different arrangement o
rooms and staircase was adopted. Houses built on a smalle
scale in lesser streets followed the same general pattern, unt
by the time the suburbs were built, in the 1820s and after, th
plain front was penetrated only by one large window on eac
floor.

Decoration of the stark, dark fronts was frequently limited t
bright reveals round the windows or perhaps a pattern of rusti
stones round the entrance, painted in a light colour to sho
up against the wall. Some houses had decorative balconie
added in iron, as in Berkeley Square or in the surviving ol
houses at the upper end of Park Lane. A change to a brighte
exterior came when John Nash put his individual stamp on th
newest and most fashionable parts of Regency London, b
introducing plaster fronts with classical details in stucc
covered in oil-paint.

Though the rows of houses built in the new squares an
streets of eighteenth-century London had a high degree o
uniformity, there were few examples of a combination o
houses in a single great architectural scheme. The Adelph
the outstanding instance of this type of project. It originate
with the Adam brothers, three of whom were architects, an
one a banker. In 1757 Robert Adam had visited Spalato (Spl
in modern Yugoslavia) and surveyed the ruins of the palace o
Diocletian, an experience which left its mark on the Adelph
scheme. Pooling their resources, in 1768 the brothers leased fo
99 years from the Duke of St Albans a piece of land calle
Durham Yard. Situated to the south of the Strand, it slope
down towards the Thames, and was occupied by small, delap

lated houses. The object was to transform this neglected area into a combination of fashionable streets of houses for wealthy London residents, standing above a complex of vaulted cellar warehouses giving on to a quay on the Thames. The houses were united into a broad block with a palace-like front and two side wings. Unfortunately for the financial success of the scheme, it proved difficult to let either the houses or the huge and costly cellars, and there was a further disappointment when the government declined to hire the latter for an arsenal. The subsequent embanking of the Thames, too, shut off the warehouses from access to the river. In the end Parliament sanctioned a special lottery with the individual houses as the prizes. There was great interest in the tickets, and so this highly speculative and imaginative scheme was saved.

The burgeoning of new building activity after the Napoleonic Wars reflected again the influence of cheaper money as well as the pressure of increasing population. It resulted in, among other things, a new *genus* of street names – the 40 or so called

A view of the Adelphi, showing the warehouses with direct access to the river. This formed an integral part of the original scheme.

after the hero Wellington and his famous battles. From the 1820s the most rapid growth was mainly to the west and south of the existing built-up area. To the north, however, the Eyre estate appeared in St John's Wood with the novelty of detached and semi-detached houses – the first estate development to abandon the Georgian terrace. West of Buckingham Palace, which had been rebuilt by George IV, the Grosvenor estate spread extensively and profitably through the fields of Pimlico. Regent's Park, too, began to emerge as 'a fairy princess's setting for the Regent's mistresses', following Nash's first definite proposals of 1811. Most of the land, some of it used for intensive hay farming, was left as open ground, with two or three hundred acres laid out as a park with isolated trees, lawns, groves and shrubberies, and the whole surrounded by a broad promenade for carriages and pedestrians. The inhabitants of the neighbouring terraces and fashionable villas could enjoy town life and still feel as though they were in the country. It was fortunate for London that the Prince was aristocratic enough to want to create a new Hyde Park for himself, since an alternative proposal would have parcelled out the whole for building small houses around squares together with cottages. In Nash's plan, however, there was also a quarter, to the east of the Park, for small houses around squares which were intended as market places. The whole scheme had been conceived as a complete 'town cell', with park, areas of housing for the well-to-do, and for those of lower incomes; and the Regent's Canal, which was included in the project, connected the new suburb with the docks and the East End.

After the appropriate Act had been passed in 1813, Nash proceeded with his further plans for linking the new Regent's Park to St James's Park in the south. A project for a main artery leading north to the open land beyond the city had been suggested by John Gwynn in 1760. He saw it as an extension of the Haymarket, running from the east end of the Mall to a new east-west avenue which would form the northern boundary of the town. His plan was never realized, but it probably influenced the Prince Regent's desire for a magnificent road leading from his residence at Carlton House (where the Duke of York's statue now stands) to his Regent's Park, as a rival to Paris's new Rue de Rivoli. The Regent's dream, fortunately, could be justified as a practical scheme for clearing away a hotch-potch of mean streets and insanitary housing, and providing a major traffic artery leading to Portland Place. (This splendid thoroughfare, 100 feet wide, bordered by its

dam houses, owed much to Lord Foley who, in building
oley House, had got the Duke of Portland to promise not to
uild on the fields and meadows to his north. The Duke,
owever, got round this difficulty by leaving a wide strip of
and, Portland Place, open from the front of Foley House to
egent's Park.)

The new Regent Street was built mainly on land belonging
o the crown, and its construction prevented the swarming
ack streets of Soho to the east from encroaching on the more
efined and fashionable neighbourhoods of Hanover Square
nd Bond Street to the west. The street's pronounced curve as
leaves Piccadilly was not in Nash's original plan, but he
ad to abandon the original straighter line for his road in
rder to avoid excessive expenses acquiring property for
development; similarly, he had to swing the northern end
round All Souls' Church and Foley House into an unchanged

The lower end of Nash's Regent Street, showing the Quadrant with its impressive arcades.

Portland Place, instead of driving a new road parallel and to the east of Portland Place. The Quadrant, built on the quarter-circle formed by the lower part of Regent Street, was perhaps the finest part of the scheme. Nash had intended to build the whole street in the style of the Quadrant, with the pavements covered by arcades reminiscent of the Rue de Rivoli, but this proved impossible. Later, in 1848, the arcades of the Quadrant were removed to give better light for the shops, for which Regent Street was becoming best known. 'Regent Street', remarks Rasmussen, 'though noble and dignified, lacked true grandeur':

> In reality it was merely a succession of dexterous solutions of difficult problems. There was never much artistic connection between the different parts. The whole was carried out according to a simple recipe: when the street crossed a main artery, a circular space was formed as in Piccadilly Circus and Oxford Circus. When the direction was to be altered or continued on parallel lines, it was terminated by a monumental building and the line was carried on by means of circular sections connecting the proper parts. While the quarters of the baroque style created open squares with conscious connection, forming a rhythmical rise and fall, Nash pieced the whole together mechanically like the plumber connecting his pipes with fittings constructed for the purpose. (*London: the Unique City*, 1937)

With the encouragement of the Prince Regent, now King George IV, Nash went on to add other landmarks to London's geography. He converted the straight canal that ran through St James's Park into a beautiful ornamental lake, built the triumphal arch and screen that dominates Hyde Park Corner, developed Pall Mall and Trafalgar Square as a fitting termination of Whitehall, and raised the National Gallery to overlook the northern perimeter of his great square.

The building of churches was a necessary but somewhat neglected corollary of London's growth. True, some planning schemes thought out by the great landowners had included new churches, but in general, as London expanded, the proportion of churches to the population declined. The target of 50 new churches envisaged by an Act of 1710 was never reached, and in the 20 years after George I came to the throne only some 29 churches were either built or rebuilt. Subsequent performance was even worse, and in 1812 it was calculated that London's 186 Anglican churches and chapels provided accommodation for only a quarter of the potential church-goers. Some areas, like Marylebone and St Pancras, were

particularly under-provided, but the shortcomings of the Church of England were made good, in part, by the more numerous foundations of the Free Churches. However, as Professor Rudé has remarked, Londoners were better off in this respect than were the inhabitants of the new industrial cities such as Liverpool, Manchester and Leeds; after 1818 the 'Million' Church Building Act, by which Parliament voted a million pounds for new churches, tilted the balance even further in London's favour.

The expansion of northern suburbs had since the middle of the eighteenth century been encouraged by the New Road, which linked Paddington and Islington; and additional bridges across the Thames led to further growth in south London. If the gentry and middle classes preferred the

Herne Hill as it appeared about the time of George IV: one of the semi-rural retreats favoured by prosperous tradesmen and professional men.

northern and western environs for their residences, the successful merchants and tradesmen of the City at first generally favoured rural outposts in Essex. However, between 1816 and 1819 three further bridges, at Vauxhall, Waterloo and Southwark, speeded up the growth of Lambeth and Camberwell, and further out, of Stockwell, Brixton, Peckham, Denmark Hill, Tulse Hill and Herne Hill. These southern outskirts were particularly favoured by prosperous London tradesmen, as well as by gentlemen in the professions. In *A Tour through England and Wales*, Defoe made much of the growth that was visible, even in his time, of Londoners' country seats in Essex, particularly at West Ham, Plaistow, Stratford, Leytonstone, Walthamstow, Woodford and Wanstead, where there had occurred an impressive increase in

> handsome large houses, from £20 a year to £60, very few under £20 a year; being chiefly for the habitations of the richest citizens, such as either are able to keep two houses, one in the country, and one in the city; or for such citizens as being rich, and having left off trade, live altogether in these neighbouring villages, for the pleasure and health of the latter part of their days.
>
> The truth of this may at least appear, in that they tell me there are no less than two hundred coaches kept by the inhabitants within the circumference of these few villages named above, besides such as are kept by accidental lodgers.

Even in Defoe's time, therefore, commuting from the country to the City was well-established. About 100 years later, in 1823, William Cobbett observed the same phenomenon, though without Defoe's enthusiasm. In his day, the stock-jobbers he despised, and the 'dark, dirty-faced, half-whiskered tax-eaters' of the hated London 'wen', were commuting by coach from as far afield as Brighton:

> The town of Brighton, in Sussex, 50 miles from the Wen, is on the seaside, and is thought by the stock-jobbers to afford a salubrious air. It is so situated that a coach, which leaves it not very early in the morning, reaches London by noon; and, starting to go back in two hours and a half afterwards, reaches Brighton not very late at night. Great parcels of stock-jobbers stay at Brighton with the women and children. They skip backward and forward on the coaches, and actually carry on stock-jobbing, in 'Change Alley, though they reside at Brighton. This place is, besides, a place of great resort with the whiskered gentry. There are not less than about twenty coaches that leave the Wen every day for this place, and there being three or four different roads, there is a great rivalship for the

custom. This sets the people to work to shorten and to level the roads; and here you see hundreds of men and horses constantly at work to make pleasant and quick travelling for the jews and jobbers. The jews and jobbers pay the turnpikes, to be sure; but they get the money from the land and labourer. They drain these, from John-a-Groat's House to the Land's End, and they lay out some of the money on the Brighton roads! (*Rural Rides*)

*Overleaf* Westminster Bridge from Lambeth, 1741.

*Below* A turnpike on the approach to London.

# 2 The Face of London

*London; that great sea whose ebb and flow
At once is deaf and loud, and on the shore
Vomits its wrecks, and still howls on for more.
Yet in its depths what treasures!*

Shelley: 'Letter to Maria Gisborne'

The eighteenth-century traveller entering London might approach the capital by a number of routes. From the east or north he passed through the bustling industrial townships of Mile End or Whitechapel, thronged with the poorer sort of artisans, many immigrants among them; or through Shoreditch and Spitalfields, past the respectable houses of the silk-weavers. Coming in from the west he might be bold enough to traverse Hounslow Heath, notorious for its highwaymen and footpads. John Byng, despite his numerous journeys, had never been robbed, but as he remarked, 'I do not attribute this so much to luck as to my observance of early hours. I neither see the use or taste the pleasure of travelling in the dark.'

Further in, the traveller would pass the Half-Way House between Kensington and Knightsbridge, a large country-style inn which, with its halted wagons and horses, brought a rustic touch to the outskirts of the capital. Similarly, the Red Lion at Paddington, close by a rude bridge over a stream, was only half a mile from the Tyburn turnpike, near the spot where Marble Arch now stands. The traveller coming from Dover would probably have spent the night at Canterbury or Rochester, and had the choice of making the whole journey by the ancient Watling Street or else taking a boat from Whitstable up the Thames. If he went by road he caught his first glimpse of St Paul's across the Surrey fields, before being swallowed up among the sounds, sights and smells of 'ill-built Southwark', full of tanners and weavers.

If he journeyed later in the eighteenth century, and he was a traveller of long standing, he would no doubt observe the transformation of the various suburbs he crossed. 'Long, lazy Lewisham', as it was once called, had become by 1788 'a smart village, and the stream is turned out of the road. At South-End, further on, there is such a pretty assemblage of water and view as might well employ a painter's time.' By this period the peripheral townships of London had become the home of 'our principal merchants, mechanics and artificers', who preferred the rural surroundings of Turnham Green, Kentish Town, Clapham or Kennington to dirty Fleet Street and Cheapside. The appearance of these expanding suburbs has been well described for us by an aristocratic visitor, the Earl of Cork:

> In these dusty retreats, where the want of London smoke is supplied by the smoke of Virginia tobacco, our chief citizens are accustomed to pass the end and the beginning of every week. Their boxes (as they are modestly called) are generally built in

a row, to resemble as much as possible the streets in London. Those edifices which stand single, and at a distance from the road, have always a summer-house at the end of a small garden; which being erected upon a wall adjoining to the highway, commands a view of every carriage, and gives the owner an opportunity of displaying his best wig to every one that passes by. A little artificial fountain, spouting water sometimes to the amazing height of four feet, and in which frogs supply the want of fishes, is one of the most exquisite ornaments in these gardens. There are besides (if the spot of ground allows sufficient space for them) very curious statues of Harlequin, Scaramouch, Pierrot, and Columbine, which serve to remind their wives and daughters of what they have seen at the playhouse. (*The Connoisseur*, 1754)

Some aspects of London's outskirts were less pleasant. Innumerable brick-kilns, 'like the scars of the smallpox', filled the air with smoke, the roads were encumbered by droves of cattle and sheep, and noisome with dung, and in the church graveyards the gaping 'poor holes' created an offensive stench, especially in sultry seasons and after rain', as they were gradually filled with corpses before being covered over.

The first impressions of the capital itself were influenced by the mood of the traveller, his expectations and the time of day. London, quiet and deserted in the early morning, was a very different thing from the noise and activity of noon. In 1802, even the nature-loving Wordsworth was moved by the early-morning view of the sleeping city seen from Westminster Bridge to pen the following lines:

> *Earth has not anything to show more fair:*
> *Dull would he be of soul who could pass by*
> *A sight so touching in its majesty:*
> *This City now doth like a garment wear*
> *The beauty of the morning: silent, bare,*
> *Ships, towers, domes, theatres, and temples lie*
> *Open unto the fields, and to the sky,*
> *All bright and glittering in the smokeless air.*
> *Never did sun more beautifully steep*
> *In his first splendour valley, rock, or hill;*
> *Ne'er saw I, never felt, a calm so deep!*
> *The river glideth at his own sweet will:*
> *Dear God! the very houses seem asleep;*
> *And all that mighty heart is lying still!*

Then, as London awoke, came the first stirrings, the first signs of the animation in store. Jonathan Swift, writing nearly 100 years earlier, takes up the theme in his poem, 'Description of the Morning' (1709):

> *Now hardly here and there a hackney-coach*
> *Appearing, show'd the ruddy morn's approach,*
> *Now Betty from her master's bed had flown,*
> *And softly crept to discompose her own;*
> *The slip-shod 'prentice from his master's door*
> *Had pared the dirt, and sprinkled round the floor;*
> *Now Moll had whirl'd her mop with dext'rous airs,*
> *Prepared to scrub the entry and the stairs.*
> *The youth with broomy stumps began to trace*
> *The kennel's edge, where wheels had worn the place.*
> *The small-coal man was heard with cadence deep,*
> *Till drown'd in shriller notes of chimney-sweep:*
> *Duns at his lordship's gate began to meet;*
> *And brick-dust Moll had scream'd through half the street.*
> *The turnkey now his flock returning sees,*
> *Duly let out a-nights to steal for fees:*
> *The watchful bailiffs take their silent stands,*
> *And school-boys lag with satchels in their hands.*

The heart of the city held many surprises for the stranger. There were indeed the occasional fine buildings, mansion, church or hospital, but more often than not the edifice was partly hidden from view by mean dwellings, grimy workshops, and dreary, blank-faced warehouses. According to the newspaper *Old England*, 'some smoaky shed' was bound to obscure even the finest facade, as if the builders 'were ashamed of having laid out their money in so *useless* a manner and so unconducive to Trade and Business'.

If we look into the Streets what a Medley of Neighbourhood do we see? Here lives a Personage of high Distinction; next Door a Butcher with his stinking Shambles! A Tallow-Chandler shall front my Lord's nice Venetian Window; and two or three brawny naked Curriers [leather-dressers] in their Pits shall face a fine Lady in her back Closet, and disturb her spiritual Thoughts: At one End of the Street shall be a Chandler's Shop to debauch all the neighbouring Maids with Gin and gossipping Tales, and at the other End perhaps a Brasier, who shall thump out a noisy Disturbance, by a Ring of Hammerers, for a Quarter of a Mile round him. In the Vicinity of some good Bishop, some good Mother frequently hangs out her Flag. The Riotous, from their filthy Accommodations of a Spring Garden Bagnio, shall echo their Bacchanalian Noise to the Devotions of the opposite Chapel, which may perhaps sue in vain for a Remedy to any BOARD. Thus we go on in England, and all this owing wholly to private Interest and Caprice. (2 July 1748)

The squeamish would be not a little horrified by the rotting heads exposed on Temple Bar, a spectacle which survived until 1773; and for some years after this, they might find pathos in a glimpse of prisoners proceeding in the cart on their last journey from Newgate to Tyburn, followed by a vociferous and highly diverted crowd. Public executions, like the public exhibition of prisoners in the pillory or the whipping of bare-backed vagrants through the street at a horse's tail, were not merely a spectacle for the mob. They were supposed to point a moral and deter others. Executions, in particular, were intended to be witnessed. 'If they do not draw spectators', remarked Dr Johnson, 'they do not answer their purpose.' And he went on: 'The public was gratified by a procession, the criminal was supported by it.'

The noise and confusion in the crowded streets might also alarm the visitor accustomed to a more placid rural existence. Carts, wagons, hackney-coaches, private chaises and sedan chairs vied for the most convenient means of passage; the drivers cursed and railed against one another, and the passers-by were showered with mud whenever it rained. In his *Amusements Serious and Comical*, Tom Brown left us this vivid description:

'Make way there', says a gouty legged Chairman, that is carrying a Punk of Quality to a Morning's Exercise; or a Bartholomew Baby Beau, newly launched out of a Chocolate House with his Pockets as empty as his brains. 'Make room there', says another fellow driving a wheelbarrow of nuts, that spoil the lungs of the City Prentices. . . . 'Stand up there you blind Dog', says a Carman. 'Will you have the Cart squeeze your guts out?' One tinker knocks, another bawls, 'Have you a brass pot, iron pot, kettle, skillet, or a frying pan to mend?' Whilst another yelps louder than Homer's Stentor, 'Two a groat and four for sixpence mackerel'. One draws his mouth up to his ears, and howls out, 'Buy my Flounders', and is followed by an old burly Drab, that screams out the sale of her mades [young skate] and her soles at the same instant.

Here a sooty chimney sweeper takes the wall of a grave alderman, and a broom man jostles the parson of the parish. There a fat greasy porter runs a trunk full butt on you, while another salutes you with a flasket of eggs and butter. 'Turn out there you country putt', says a bully with a sword two yards long jarring at his heels, and throws him into the Kennel [gutter] . . .

Blind beggars and youthful sweepers outside the Horse Guards.

Traffic congestion in London was no new problem in the eighteenth century. As early as 1601 the House of Commons had passed a Bill 'to restrain the excessive and superfluous use of coaches'. The streets had become even more impassable after 1624 when the hackney coaches appeared, and the introduction a few years later of the sedan chair, intended to have the good effect of reducing coach traffic, made little impression on the hurried confusion which slowed the passage of wheeled vehicles. Broad-wheel wagons, made compulsory by law in order to protect road surfaces from excessive damage, were a real menace in the narrow streets of the city. These wagons, and the long-distance coaches as well, usually had six horses in order to cope with the mud and ruts of the country roads, which made them even more difficult to manage in the twisting, overcrowded thoroughfares of the capital. In the later part of the eighteenth century new roads and bridges offered some relief: the New Road (now the Marylebone, Euston and Pentonville roads), sanctioned in 1756, ran east and west through the fields to the north of the built-up area, and with its 40-foot carriageway provided good access on that side of the capital. But, in general, the growth of the city and of its raffic rapidly overtook such advances.

Another hazard in the streets were the numerous messenger boys, apprentices, milkmaids, stallkeepers and beggars who were only too ready to leave their concerns for any more interesting diversion. John Byng, no lover of the London crowds, tells how in Tichfield Street the mere harnessing of a horse gave rise to much 'larned advice from ignorant and out of danger spectators'.

At length the coach traveller arrived at his inn. In London a number of well-known inns in various parts of the city were the headquarters for the different coach and wagon routes, and a journey into the provinces began at one or other of these inyards – the equivalent of the modern railway station or bus depot. The coachmasters provided regular scheduled services, and the name painted on their coaches represented the service and not an individual coach, such as, for instance, the Shrewsbury *Wonder* or its rival the *Nimrod*. The greatest coachmaster

'The Arrival': coach passengers being shown into an inn, by Rowlandson.

43

in the 1830s was William Chaplin, who operated services out
of five London inns, the two best-known being the Spread
Eagle in Gracechurch Street, and the Swan with Two Necks
near Gresham Street. Chaplin's sizeable enterprise included
1,300 horses, 60 coaches and 2,000 employees. Another
famous yard, that of the Bull and Mouth, stood opposite the
General Post Office, and so was convenient for the mails. These
famous inns carried on an enormous traffic, and their accommodation had to be extensive in order to provide adequate
room for both horses and passengers. The bedrooms were built
along galleries over the stables, and even the entrance to the
yard was usually built over. With their numerous ostlers,
horsekeepers, waiters and servants, these inns provided a great
deal of employment, and they swarmed, too, with pedlars
and sightseers. Around the capital was a ring of coaching
centres, where horses were changed, and passengers might get
a few minutes' repose from the bumping and swaying. Among
the most important were Barnet, and also Hounslow, where the
Exeter, Bath and Gloucester roads joined. At Hounslow,
stabling was provided for 2,500 horses.

A coach about to set out, as seen b
Hogarth (1747). The bustle of th
coaching inns provided some live
scenes in eighteenth-century London

To stay at a coaching inn was too 'low' for the more genteel
kind of visitor, who soon found himself a suitable lodging.
When James Boswell came to London in November 1762, he
stopped at first at the Black Lion in Water Lane, Fleet Street:
'the noise, the crowd, the glare of shops and signs agreeably
confused me.' To choose a lodging proved difficult, but after
seeing some 50 or so he settled on one in Downing Street,
Westminster:

I took a lodging up two pair of stairs with the use of a handsome
parlour all the forenoon, for which I agreed to pay forty guineas
a year, but I took it for a fortnight first, by way of a trial. I also
made bargain that I should dine with the family whenever I
pleased, at a shilling a time. My landlord was Mr Terrie,
chamber-keeper to the Office for Trade and Plantations. He was
originally from the shire of Moray. He had a wife but no children.
The street was a genteel street, within a few steps of the Parade;
near the House of Commons, and very healthful.

Before long, however, Boswell felt the need for economy, and
thought of moving to a cheaper residence in Crown Street,
Westminster:

I thought my present lodgings too dear, and therefore looked
about and found a place in Crown Street, Westminster, an
obscure street but pretty lodgings at only £22 a year. Much did
I ruminate with regard to lodgings. Sometimes I considered
that a fine lodging denoted a man of great fashion, but then I
thought that few people would see it and therefore the expense
would be hid, whereas my business was to make as much show
as I could with my small allowance. I thought that an elegant
place to come home to was very agreeable and would inspire me
with ideas of my own dignity; but then I thought it would be
hard if I had not a proportionable show in other things, and
that it was better to come gradually to a fine place than from a
fine to a worse. I therefore resolved to take the Crown Street
place, and told my present landlord that I intended to leave
him. (F. A. Pottle, ed., *Boswell's London Journal, 1762–3*)

While seeking lodgings, the visitor might well be surprised
at the great variety of internal plans that the apparently
uniform terraced exteriors concealed. What Sir John Summerson called 'the insistent verticality of the London house'
produced a 'vertical living idiom'. In these narrow-fronted
houses one floor was for eating, another for sleeping, a third
for company, a fourth below street level for the kitchen, and
perhaps a fifth at the top for the servants. Louis Simond, a
French visitor to the capital, found that the agility with which
the inhabitants ran up and down and perched on the different

storeys gave 'the idea of a cage with its sticks and birds
Within this vertical framework there were many minor vari
tions – in the turn of the stairs, their rising from a hall or in
well, the double doors and recesses, and extension of the roo
by additions at the back. The differences in floor levels we
also noticeable: the front basement gave on to an 'area' reache
by steps leading down from the pavement above, with storag
for coal built out under the pavement for ease of delivery; whi
the back on the basement level led out to a yard or court, an
then by only a few steps up to the garden.

Boswell thought that London appealed to the person
imagination and feeling. London, he said,

> is undoubtedly a place where men and manners may be seen
> to the greatest advantage. The liberty and the whim that reign
> there occasions a variety of perfect and curious characters. The
> the immense crowd and hurry and bustle of business and
> diversion, the great number of public places of entertainment,
> the noble churches and the superb buildings of different kinds,
> agitate, amuse, and elevate the mind. Besides the satisfaction o
> pursuing whatever plan is most agreeable, without being know
> or looked at, is very great. Here a young man of curiosity and
> observation may have a sufficient fund of present entertainmen
> and may lay up ideas to employ his mind in age.

The town was best seen on foot. In the middle of the eigh
eenth century the west or 'court' end was soon traversed. Th
western end of Oxford Street, then called Tyburn Road, wa
edged on the north by fields. Tyburn gallows, near the site
the later Marble Arch, marked the end of the streets and house
while Hyde Park stretched out to the west of Tyburn Lane, lat
Park Lane. In Tyburn Lane was Lord Chesterfield's hous
within earshot of the noisy crowds attending the execution
From the turnpike gate at Hyde Park Corner the visitor coul
walk through Green Park, past Buckingham House, and o
by the 'stinking' canal in St James's Park. From there, if h
were staying in Boswell's lodgings, the visitor would soon b
back at home. In January 1763, Boswell himself walked to th
City from Hyde Park Corner; then he and his companion
'had an excellent breakfast at the Somerset Coffee-house . .
turned down Gracechurch Street and went upon the top
London Bridge, from whence we viewed with a pleasing horro
the rude and terrible appearance of the river, partly froze u
partly covered with enormous shoals of floating ice which ofte
crashed against each other.'

Further excursions were needed to give the newcomer
closer acquaintance with the varied aspects of London life. H

ould find, for a start, that the street names were not a little misleading: Broad Street, St Giles, was but 'a poor narrow ook'; even the ghost of a Duke could not be found in Duke's lace; and Brook Street possessed no refreshing stream. A isit to some of the famous squares in the last years of the entury would show signs of change. Soho and Golden Squares vere already unfashionable, and their desertion by the aristoc-acy had led to invasion by commercial interests. Professor Rudé tells us that as early as 1742 Joseph Mahoon, a maker of arpsichords, had set up business in Golden Square, to be ollowed in due course by an army contractor and a firm of vholesalers. Soho Square continued to be a genteel address for ome time. But its gentry, dowagers, Members of Parliament nd professional men were joined around 1785 by an army ontractor who converted three houses into a warehouse, which n 1815 became the Soho Bazaar. Nearby Leicester Square was osing its distinguished residences of the country gentry as rofessional men, especially doctors, moved in, accompanied y Barker's Panorama and Mary Linwood's gallery of needle-

Buckingham House, and St James's Park with its 'stinking canal', as they appeared in 1741.

*Overleaf* Covent Garden, showing St Paul's Church, the 'handsomest barn in England', and the extensive market which caused the more fastidious residents to seek quieter quarters.

47

work. Elsewhere, Hanover Square became another resort for the professional classes, and the Duke of Bedford 'deserted Bedford House and Bloomsbury Square to make way for his new "middling" tenants in 1810'. Of the older fashionable areas, only St James's 'retained something of its hold on the aristocracy'.

Covent Garden Piazza, the first real London square, had long been in decline, though on 1 March 1730 the *Morning Advertiser* announced:

> The Lady Wortley Montagu, who has been greatly indisposed at her house in Covent Garden for some time, is now perfectly recovered, and takes the benefit of the air in Hyde Park every morning by advice of her physicians.

Inigo Jones's church of St Paul's – 'the handsomest barn in England', as he described it to the Earl of Bedford (in response to the Earl's demand for a cheap church, little better than a barn) – dominated the Piazza by its sheer simplicity and force. The large portico facing on to the Piazza did not in fact form the entrance to the church but was really, as Rasmussen has said, a sort of forum or gathering place, where the Members of Parliament for Westminster were elected. But from an early date the genteel residents of the Piazza and its neighbourhood began moving out. The Turkish Bath established there at the beginning of the nineteenth century probably did not improve its attractions as a residential area. An advertisement announced:

> At the Hummum's in Covent Garden are the best accommodation for Persons of Quality to sweat or bath every day in the week, the conveniences of all kinds far exceeding all other Bagnios or Sweating Houses both for Rich and Poor. Persons of good reputation may be accommodated with handsome lodgings to lie all night. There is also a man and a woman who cups [bleeds with a cup] after the newest and easiest method. In the garden of the same house is also a large cold bath of spring water, which, for its coldness and delicacy, deserves an equal reputation with any in use.

The daily vegetable market, established in 1671, soon spread into the neighbouring streets, making the early mornings resound with rumbling cart-wheels and shouting porters, and leaving behind an odorous debris of rotting cabbage leaves and overripe fruit. From midnight the streets were blocked by market-gardeners' wagons from Lewisham or Plumstead, and in due course the stalls and sheds which filled the square were transformed into permanent market halls. Yet a further

Cheapside with the church of St Mary-Le-Bow, about 1750. Note the large and numerous shop signs.

50

disadvantage of Covent Garden from the residential point of view was the unsavoury reputation it acquired for robberies and assaults.

As the visitor penetrated beyond Covent Garden into the commercial and industrial heart of the city, he could hardly fail to be impressed by the many squalid sights and sounds that assailed the senses. Fleet Bridge was a spot to be passed quickly

51

in order to escape the appalling stench of the River Fleet, really an open sewer, its murky waters drifting turgidly to mingle with the Thames. In this district the stranger was confronted by what a contemporary called 'the hotchpotch of half-moon and serpentine narrow streets, close, dismal, long lanes, stinking allies, dark gloomy courts and suffocating yards'. The mud-spattered pavements were obstructed by heaps of building materials and casks, and by carts and wagons drawn partly off the roadway, as well as piles of rubbish; the open holes let into the pavements for the delivery of coal, barrels, and other merchandise provided further hazards for the unwary. In rainy weather the gutter spouts, in the absence of drainpipes, sent down streams of water not quite clear of the pavement. Pedestrians jostled to 'take the wall', meaning to secure the inside of the pavement out of reach of water cascading from the roofs. In 'Trivia' (1716), John Gay, no stranger to the dangers of London town, proposed the following precepts for the pedestrian:

> When waggish boys the stunted beesom ply
> To rid the slabby pavement; pass not by
> E'er thou has held their hands; some heedless flirt
> Will over-spread thy calves with spatt'ring dirt.
> Where porters hogsheads roll from carts aslope,
> Or brewers down steep cellars stretch the rope,
> Where counted billets are by carmen tost;
> Stay thy rash step, and walk without the post.
>
> Where Lincolns Inn, wide space, is rail'd around
> Cross not with vent'rous step; there oft is found
> The lurking thief, who while the day-light shone,
> Made the walls echo with his begging tone;
> That crutch which late compassion mov'd, shall wound
> Thy bleeding head, and fell thee to the ground.
> Though thou art tempted by the linkman's call,
> Yet trust him not along the lonely wall;
> In the mid-way he'll quench the flaming brand,
> And share the booty with the pilf'ring band.
> Still keep the publick streets where oily rays
> Shot from the crystal lamp, o'erspread the ways.

In this part of London, amidst the dirt and 'slop of the streets', were found itinerant hawkers with their trays of trifles, stalls of fruit, vegetables, pots and pans, and wandering exhibitions of performing dogs and donkeys, bears, giants, dwarfs, and similar sources of amazement. A procession or a

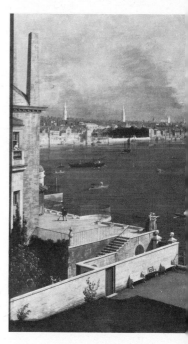

*Top* Congestion in Pall Mall, as seen by Rowlandson, 1807.

street fair was not an uncommon sight. On May Day there would be a good chance of seeing the milkmaids carrying through the streets their 'garland' of flowers arranged in a pyramid some seven or eight tiers high, and garnished at the corners with objects of silver: tea-kettles, urns or jugs, borrowed for the occasion. On that day, too, the chimney sweeps danced in the streets, their soot-grimed faces whitened with flour and their clothes decked out with ribbons and lace. A violinist recruited for the merry-making dragged tunes from his instrument while the sweeps accompanied him with bangs and crashes from their brushes and scrapers, pausing now and again to beg a little money from the gawping onlookers.

Among the things which might literally strike the stranger were the street signs, often so inconveniently large that they stuck out right across the pavement and excluded the daylight from the narrower streets and alleys. Addison complained in *The Spectator*, No 28, that many of these signs bore no relation to the trade carried on inside. 'A Cook should not live at the Boot, nor a Shoemaker's at the Roasted Pig; and yet, for want of this regulation, I have seen a Goat set up before the door of a Perfumer, and the French King's Head at a Sword-Cutler's.' Streets often had no name signs, and were unnumbered. Those whose names the visitor did discover might remind him of medieval markets: Bread Street, Milk Street and Poultry. There was Cannon Street, named after the candlemakers who once worked there, and Threadneedle Street, named for the Needlemakers Company, though possibly also after a children's game. There was also Grub Street, in St Giles, Cripplegate, within hailing distance of Bedlam and the pestilential marshes of Moorfields. Inhabited by poor, struggling writers, it was a mean district, and a disreputable one too. At the Royal Exchange the visitor might notice with surprise that the pillars were adorned with advertisements, and that the entrance was cluttered with stalls like a market, 'selling cures for your corns, glass eyes for the blind, ivory teeth for broken mouths, and spectacles for the weak-sighted; the passage to the gate being lined with hawkers, gardeners, mandrake sellers, and porters... a pippin monger's stall, surmounted with a chemist's shop where drops, elixirs, cordials and balsams had justly the pre-eminence of apples, chestnuts, pears and oranges.'

On his return to the West End, the visitor would notice with relief how much wider, cleaner and certainly less dangerous were the streets; and if it were some time after 1762, the date of the Westminster Paving Act, they would also be far smoother underfoot. Flat stones replaced the pebbles, and raised causeways provided a dry crossing for pedestrians, to the discomfort of those in carriages. Gutters on each side of the street replaced the old central kennel (channel); and the accumulated jungle of posts, stones, doorsteps, shop signs and other obstructions had been cleared away. Before the end of the century the new thoroughfares were lit by oil lamps erected on iron posts with two, three, and sometimes four branches bearing large glass globes. A foreign visitor, W. de Archenholtz, noted that 'they are lighted at sunset, both in winter and summer, as well when the moon shines as not. In Oxford Street alone, there are more lamps than in all Paris.'

But despite the stranger's surprise these lights were not really very efficient, and were replaced in due course by the more effective gas lighting, much to the alarm and dismay of the 'harpy set of painted harlots' who frequented Bond Street and the Haymarket. As early as 1807, the south side of Pall Mall was illuminated by 13 gas lamps, and the Gas Light and Coke Company, incorporated in 1812, established its first gasworks in Great Peter Street, Westminster.

Pall Mall, Kensington Gardens, and the Mall by St James's Park, were the resorts of fashionable Londoners on Sunday, while the 'common people' made for St George's Fields, Greenwich Park, Marylebone Gardens or Highgate. Parks, as Lord Chatham remarked, were 'the lungs of London'. Among the fashionable ones, Kensington Gardens soon became the most exclusive after it was fenced round and servants were placed at the entrances to prevent 'persons meanly clad' from entering. St James's Park had been improved by Charles II, who is reputed to have summoned the famous landscape gardener Le Nôtre from Paris to advise on laying it out. It was said that Le Nôtre thought the Park's natural simplicity, 'its rural, and in some places, wild character, had something more grand than he could impart to it, and persuaded the King not to touch it'. The Mall, however, was laid out as a broad avenue, with four lines of trees, not as a stately approach to Buckingham House, but as a place where the merry monarch could indulge in pall mall (vulgarly known as pell-mell), a game in which a ball was struck by a mallet through arches at each end of an alley.

Fanny Burney was much impressed by the fine company to be seen in the Mall in her day: 'Everybody looked gay, and seemed pleased and the ladies were so much dressed, that Mrs Mirvan and I could do nothing but look at them.' But the Mall itself was a disappointment: 'A long straight walk, of dirty gravel, very uneasy to the feet; and at each end, instead of an

The rustic character of London 'lungs' is well illustrated by this scene of an airing in Hyde Park, 1798.

pen prospect, nothing is to be seen but houses built of brick. When Mrs Mirvan pointed out the *Palace* to me – I think I was ever much more surprised.' Nevertheless, the Mall and St ames's Park, like Kensington Gardens, Hyde Park, and the arer Pall Mall, offered a pleasant escape from the hubbub the city streets, as John Gay reminds us in 'Trivia':

> *O bear me to the paths of fair Pell-mell;*
> *Safe are thy pavements, grateful is thy smell!*
> *At distance rolls along the gilded coach,*
> *Nor sturdy carmen on thy walks encroach;*
> *No lets would bar thy ways were chairs deny'd*
> *The soft supports of laziness and pride;*
> *Shops breathe perfumes, thro' sashes ribbons glow,*
> *The mutual arms of ladies, and the beau.*
> *Yet still ev'n here, when rains the passage hide,*
> *Oft the loose stone spirts up a muddy tide*

*Beneath thy careless foot; and from on high*
*Where masons mount the ladder fragments fly;*
*Mortar, and crumbled lime in show'rs descend,*
*And o'er thy head destructive tiles impend.*

Fanny Burney admired the high fashion to be seen in th
Mall if not the Mall itself. Indeed the quality of Londoner
dress often surprised foreign visitors such as Archenholtz. Th
English 'luxury of dress', he wrote in the 1780s, surpassed tha
of all other nations:

> Twenty years ago, neither gold nor silver were to be seen on a
> coat, except at court or the theatre. Persons in dress went in
> carriages; on foot they never wore swords, and the *petits maîtres*
> put on their hats. This last custom remains, but all the rest are
> changed. Even the common people have embroidered vests.
> Everybody in summer as well as in winter wears a plain coat bu
> of the finest cloth; no tradesman will wear anything else. No

furs are used, but great surtouts which protect from the rain in summer, and the cold in winter. In this simple dress do the first ministers of state walk the streets of London, without being followed by a single servant . . . Nobody, even among the common people, wears a turned coat, or a soled shoe. Shirts of the finest linen are generally worn, and even the lower sort have a clean one every day. The cleanliness of the English in everything is admirable. (*A View of the British Constitution and of the Manners and Customs of the People of England*)

Our visitor to eighteenth-century London has so far made only a preliminary investigation of the sights of the city. But there was still much to explore beyond the mere outward appearance of the streets and their inhabitants – the coffee houses, inns, and clubs, the pleasure gardens and theatres, and it is to these further aspects of Georgian London that we turn next.

'The Entrance to the Mall', a water-colour by Rowlandson. The Mall provided a popular promenade for the fashionable where, said Fanny Burney, 'everybody looked gay and seemed pleased'.

A mingled gathering crowds the walks in Vauxhall Gardens, in this water-colour by Rowlandson. The gardens were sited just south-east of the present railway station.

# 3 Society's London

'No, Sir, when a man is tired of London, he is tired of life: for
there is in London all that life can afford.'

Dr Johnson

As we noted in Chapter 1, the great squares of London wer created by the aristocracy, who took advantage of their ow creations to provide themselves with London residences. / succession of builders and architects were employed to produc houses for the landed proprietors in a variety of styles – Dutcl at the time of Queen Anne, Italian and French during th reigns of the first Georges, and subsequently the long-popula Palladian design. Many names famous in the history c architecture were involved – Kent, Ware, Gibbs, Danc Hawksmoor, Holland, and especially the Adam brothers, wh built houses for the Earl of Bute, the Duke of Buckingham an Lord Stanley. The houses were designed to suit the kind of lif that aristocratic families led in town: impressive dining room for elaborate suppers, stately ballrooms for the glittering rou or party, more modest anterooms for the occasional salon private conference or interview.

Coming up to London for the season, as the wealthie country landowners did, was an expensive business. Ther was the upkeep of the house, servants, entertaining and horse to say nothing of the theatres and pleasure gardens, and th temptations of the shops. A stay in London could strain th pockets of even the richest of the aristocracy. The Duke c Kingston spent over £2,000 during a mere fortnight's stay i the summer of 1752, and a still larger sum in the followin winter, when his bills included £379 from his wine merchan £197 for stabling his horses and £101 for coal. Lord Ash burnham, who came up regularly from Sussex, incurred perso nal expenditure of nearly £26,000 over a period of six year between 1710 and 1716, spending an average of over £4,000 year on his family's annual stay in the capital. The Duke c Bedford kept over 40 servants at his London house, and thei wages alone amounted to £860 annually – in an era whe chambermaids and parlour maids could be hired for a fev pounds a year. These amounts strike us as tremendous ever today, when inflation has greatly blunted the impact of larg sums, and the £5-note is as familiar as only the £1-note wa not many years ago. It is hard to appreciate the magnitude c these eighteenth-century outlays until one remembers that few hundred pounds a year was a very comfortable middle class income – many country gentlemen lived on less – an that the average labourer probably did not see more tha about £30 for a whole year's work.

Entertaining was then, as now, extremely costly if mounte on anything like a lavish scale: the first Duke of Devonshir once spent £1,000 on a supper and masked ball. Not ever occasion was lavish, of course, but a great deal of entertaining was done throughout the London season. James Boswell recorded in his diary how, on 7 December 1762, he went to Lord Eglinton's:

> Where was a breakfast, a concert, and a most elegant company: the Prince of Mecklenburg, Duke of Kingston, Duke of Portland, Duke and Duchess of Ancaster, Duchess of Hamilton, Lord Lorne, Lord March, Lord Lichfield, Chancellor of the University of Oxford, Lord and Lady Garlies, Lady Margaret Macdonald, Mr Harris, author of the essays on Poetry, Music, and Happiness, and a great many more. It was really a fine thing. Since ever I came up, I have resolved to preserve my own dignity and pay court to nobody, and rather have no communication with people than in any degree cringe to them. This morning I could observe Sir James Macdonald waiting till I should make up to him, which I did not do, but sat down by myself. He came and sat down beside me, and we chatted very well. I said I should wish to pass an hour or two with him. He said he would come and see me. This interview was very pleasing to me.

The very same evening Boswell went to a rout at Northumberland House:

> Which was indeed magnificent. Three large rooms and the gallery (a prodigious one) were full of the best company, between three and four hundred of them. The gallery is like one of the rooms in Holyroodhouse for size and richly adorned on the walls and ceiling with landscapes and gilding. The King and Lady Northumberland are exhibited in full length portraits, in their robes.

Not everyone obtained the *entrée* to fashionable society as did Boswell. Many of the undistinguished and less well-heeled country gentry visited London only very occasionally, more for purposes of business than pleasure. When they did they would make do with a rented house or lodgings, and mix only with relations and friends of their own sort. The more eminent gentry who were Members of Parliament came up regularly, of course, to attend the House. Sir Thomas Chester, Member for Gloucestershire, paid four guineas a week for family lodgings in Golden Square, and his family party set out on their four-days' journey to the capital well provided in cash with £161 in notes and £149 in coins – rich pickings for the highwayman. Perhaps they took the precaution of secreting the money in a goose or parcel, as Walpole's steward did when he sent his master's Norfolk rents to London. Sir Thomas needed all his money and more, for his four-months' stay ran

Having one's portrait painted was almost *de rigueur* for the wealthy in Georgian London. Here is Robert Walpole in the studio of Francis Hayman (from the painting by Francis Hayman, R.A., *c.* 1740–45).

away with £371 for lodgings and housekeeping, while a furthe £384 was required to meet bills for clothes, wine (£51), mea (£31), coal (£15) and candles (£4 14s). Clothes figured larg in the spending of London visitors, for a visit to the capita offered the opportunity of replacing one's wardrobe with th latest fashions. Similarly, it was the time to restock one's win cellar, order a new coach, augment one's library, and acquir musical instruments and jewellery. In 1712–13, for instance Sir Walter Calverley, up from Yorkshire, spent £260 o furniture and a new 'chariot'. Lord Ashburnham purchase 77 gallons of white wine for 38s 6d to be sent down to Susse as well as 63 gallons of cider, with bottles and corks, for £8 At the same time some pamphlets for his library, including 'Mr Halley's Description of the Eclipse', came to only 2s.

Lord Ashburnham, like many other wealthy noblemen an gentry, had his portrait painted – £44 10s – during one visi to London. London boasted a large colony of artists, and durin the Georgian period English painters gradually superseded the Dutch and French ones in aristocratic favour. Sir Godfrey Kneller was the first of the great Georgian painters to make his mark, but later the list of successful English artists included Hogarth, Gainsborough, Reynolds and George Romney. The Royal Academy was founded in 1769, with Reynolds as its first President, and George III set an example in giving his patronage to British artists. By 1760 Reynolds was charging 25 guineas for a head – he had asked only five guineas a few years earlier – and Gainsborough, in 1786, could demand 40 guineas, and 160 guineas for a full-length portrait.

Obtaining expert medical attention was also best done in London. The eminent physicians of the early Georgian age, Garth, Arbuthnot, Sloane, Meade, Freind, Radcliffe and Fothergill, charged enormous fees, and made some £5,000–6,000 a year. William Chiselden, the great surgeon and anatomist, was celebrated for the 'lateral operation for the stone', which he could perform almost painlessly in 54 seconds. He was also a gifted designer, and prepared the plans for the first Putney Bridge. In 1741 William Hunter came to London, and with his brother John set up a medical school in Windmill Street. William developed a flourishing practice in midwifery, while John studied comparative anatomy. However, there were a great many entirely bogus quacks about, amateur surgeons, oculists, bone-setters and pill-makers. The Chevalier Taylor, who professed to have a cure for blindness, was described by Dr Johnson as 'an instance how far impudence could carry ignorance', and Joshua Ward, who made a fortune from his antimony pill, was patronized by Lord Chesterfield, Horace Walpole and George II.

Shopping was one of the great occupations in London, for even if a provincial gentleman came to town alone, he was sure to be burdened with numerous commissions on behalf of his family and neighbours. Dudley North, a Member of Parliament for Suffolk, was reminded by his bailiff of his daughter's request for a 'Quilted petty Coat', while Nicholas Blundell, a modest Lancashire squire, had much to do in ordering his wedding clothes in the May of 1703. He purchased $5\frac{1}{8}$ yards of blue cloth at 18s per yard, 16 yards of durrance for linings at 1s 3d, $3\frac{3}{4}$ dozen silver buttons at 7s 6d a dozen, and 5 dozen silver breast buttons at 2s; and the tailor himself was paid £1 15s 'for making this my Wedding Sute'. Blundell completed his outfit with a pair of scarlet stockings at 10s, and two sets of livery for his grooms costing £9 3s 5d. Presents for his bride included six 'gilt Coffy Spoones' bought for 18s, a

Fashionable shoppers study the display at a print shop in St Paul's Churchyard, oblivious of the arrest being made right next to them (1774).

'fals Diamond Necklase' for £1 1s 6d, a 'fals Diamond Ring' for 14s; his own wedding ring cost £1 5s. The London shops were cautious in extending credit to strangers, but Boswell managed to buy a sword on trust, as he recalls in his diary entry for 1 December 1762:

On Tuesday I wanted to have a silver-hilted sword, but upon examining my pockets as I walked up the Strand, I found that I had left the most of my guineas at home and had not enough to pay for it with me. I determined to make a trial of the civility of my fellow-creatures, and what effect my external appearance and address would have. I accordingly went to the shop of Mr Jefferys, sword-cutter to his Majesty, looked at a number of his swords, and at last picked out a very handsome one at five guineas. 'Mr Jefferys,' said I, 'I have not money here to pay for it. Will you trust me?' 'Upon my word, Sir,' said he, 'you must excuse me. It is a thing we never do to a stranger.' I bowed genteely and said, 'Indeed, Sir, I believe it is not right.' However, I stood and looked at him, and he looked at me. 'Come, Sir,' cried he, 'I will trust you.' 'Sir,' said I, 'if you had not trusted me, I should not have bought it from you.' He asked my name and place of abode, which I told him. I then chose a belt, put the sword on, told him I would call and pay it tomorrow, and walked off. I called this day and paid him. 'Mr Jefferys,' said I, 'there is your money. You paid me a very great compliment. I am much obliged to you. But pray don't do such a thing again. It is dangerous.' 'Sir,' said he, 'we know our men. I would have trusted you with the value of a hundred pounds.' This I think was a good adventure and much to my honour.

Of course those London shopkeepers who had dealings with the nobility and gentry were accustomed to extending long credit, and indeed they sometimes had to wait years for their bills to be settled. There was a strong tendency for the aristocracy to spend beyond their immediate means, and the complicated finances of landed proprietors often meant that the amount of ready money available to them was severely restricted. The fashionable London shops, presumably, allowed for all this in their prices, and certainly they were adept at flattering the ladies with a judicious display of elegance and luxury. Thomas Baker makes this clear in his account of a shopping expedition which he undertook:

We went into a shop which had three partners; two of them were to flourish out their silks, and after an obliging smile and a pretty mouth made Cicero-like, to expatiate on their goodness; and the other's sole business was to be gentleman

Cruikshank's view of Londoners amusing themselves on Primrose Hill, 179

64

usher of the shop, to stand completely dressed at the door, bow to all the coaches that pass by, and hand ladies out and in. We saw abundance of gay fancies, fit for sea-captains' wives, sheriffs' feasts, and Taunton-dean ladies. 'This, madam, is wonderful charming. This, madam, is so diverting a silk. This, madam, my stars! how cool it looks! But this, madam – ye Gods! would I had 10,000 yards of it!' Then gathers up a sleeve, and places it to our shoulders. 'It suits your ladyship's face wonderfully well.' When we had pleased ourselves, and bid him ten shillings a-yard for what he asked fifteen: 'Fan me, ye winds, your ladyship rallies me! Should I part with it at such a price, the weavers would rise upon the very shop. Was you at the Park last night, madam? Your ladyship shall abate me sixpence. Have you read the *Tatler* to-day?' (*The Female Tatler*, 1709)

While the ladies shopped, or prepared for the next rout or supper party, the gentlemen attended Parliament, visited their lawyers to discuss family settlements and mortgages, and talked money with their bankers. For many of them London was more costly than amusing. John Byng thought it sad that comfortable country gentlemen should ruin their fortunes and their health by removal to the capital. He was inclined to blame the ladies for this misfortune:

Is not this the case every day? How comfortable long and happy might gentry reside at their own good houses in the country: and perhaps, for some years, some do; till madame, getting the upper hand, and urging the old motives of education for the girls and of stirring interest for the boys, drives the unhappy unresisting husband to crawl through his shortened, latter days, miserably, in a dog hole in Marylebone parish!

A well-spent country life should consist in farming, gardening, fishing, riding, and in reading old and new authors – what more man is to be wished for? For all the rest is scandal, folly, madness! Even the littleness of country sports exceed, surely, the wicked idleness of London occupations? (*Torrington Diaries*)

But the London season, with all its extravagance, formed an essential element in the lives of the wealthy, and could not be escaped without a serious loss of prestige and influence; for it was the months in London, as much as the country mansion and estate, which proclaimed membership of the more exclusive circles of society. Only by mixing in the grand London *milieu* could one have any hope of gaining personal preferment, of 'stirring interest' for one's sons, as Byng said, or of securing a suitable match for one's rather too plain daughters. And even in London it was still possible to engage in country pursuits. The capital was still small enough for the countryside to be within easy reach. Chalk Farm was still a farm, and there were hay-fields between Paddington and Bayswater. There were, too, the London parks with their amenities for riding, walking and ball games. In the suburbs bowling greens were popular among both the young and the not-so-young. Putney, Hoxton, Marylebone, Hampstead, Stoke Newington and Ham Lane all had greens, as did many other places. There were spas, too, quite near at hand, in particular the mildly chalybeate spring at Hampstead. Concerts were held both there and at Richmond Wells when the season opened in May. At Epsom, favoured by the aristocracy, the season began earlier, on Easter Monday, and again there was music as well as shops, performing dogs, morris dancing, and eventually the horse-racing for which the town became most famous. Various places advertised the value of their medicinal springs, and the waters were bottled to be sold more widely; among these were Acton waters, Streatham, Dulwich, Sydenham Wells, Lambeth Wells, Sadler's New Tunbridge Wells at Islington, and the 'London Spa at the sign of the Fountain in the parish of St James's Clerkenwell (the poor may have it gratis)'.

Angling at Sadler's Wells, one of th local spas favoured by Londoner 1796.

Mr Bovill, in his book *English Country Life*, tells us that even hunting impinged upon, and sometimes involved, the capital'. The Old Berkeley hounds hunted right up to Kensington Gardens, while round Croydon, known as 'the Melton of the South', there was a choice of three packs of foxhounds, two of harriers, as well as the Surrey and Lord Derby's staghounds. Staghounds also hunted the country around Hounslow and Twickenham, where Lord Alvanley complained that the melon and asparagus beds in the market gardens made the going 'devilish heavy . . . up to our hocks in glass all day'.

Another outdoor interest that could be pursued in London was gardening. The area to the west of the city was noted for its nurseries offering large selections of native and exotic trees and shrubs. Commercial nurseries were certainly established before the end of the seventeenth century. In the 1680s, Roger Looker, the Queen's gardener, and his partners founded a large nursery extending over 50 acres at Brompton Park in Kensington. Other nurseries were established in the environs of London, by a Mr Cox of Kew Green near Richmond, a Mr Masters at Strand-on-the-Green near Brentford, and a Mr Mason at Isleworth. In 1772 Cox had over 30,000 plants at Kew, including elms, hornbeams, horse chestnuts, sycamores and limes, while Mason's stock showed a trend towards Scots and silver firs and spruce. In addition Cox stocked specimens of barberry, box, Spanish broom, honeysuckle, Persian jasmine, laurel, lilac and syringa. Among fruit trees, pears, apples, peaches, nectarines, plums and cherries were popular, as well as currant, gooseberry and mulberry bushes. The eighteenth-century fashion for landscaping influenced the market considerably, the nursery business expanded, and specialist nurserymen provided new and exotic shrubs such as andromedas, magnolias and rhododendrons. Published catalogues, running to 60 or 70 pages, made their appearance in the 1770s, and among the leading London firms to issue them were James Gordon, William Malcolm, Kennedy and Lee, and Conrad Loddiges of Hackney. Returning in 1768 from his northern tour, Arthur Young noted that 'good nursery land' at Hammersmith rented for 'from £2 to £4 in general, and to £6 if walled. The nurseries rise from five to fifty acres. One of twenty acres will employ from eight to ten hands constantly, at 10s 6d a week in summer, and 9s in winter.'

Very fashionable in the mid eighteenth century, and for a long time after, were the pleasure gardens of Ranelagh at Chelsea, and Vauxhall on the south side of the river. There society congregated for the music, brilliant lights, interesting company, balls, masquerades and fireworks. Vauxhall beautiful walks, entrance fee only a shilling up to 1792, ha grottoes, statues, temples and waterfalls, and were noted as rendezvous for all kinds of intrigue. At the Spring Gardens, Vauxhall was known until 1785, supper was served in litt kiosks built in Chinese style, while Ranelagh, though lackir in 'dark walks', boasted its Rotunda, a round hall some 15 feet in diameter. Ranelagh was the more aristocratic of th two, and served no suppers or wine. It was also the mor expensive, although its 2s 6d admission charge included te and coffee. Ranelagh gave Dr Johnson 'an expansion and ga sensation to my mind, such as I never experienced anywher else'. The Rotunda's curving walls were divided into thre storeys: the first containing boxes each with a table and seats fo ten persons; the boxes of the second tier had the addition movable lattices to provide privacy, should it be required; an the top was a large gallery holding an organ and a choir. Th great and fashionable mixed with lesser mortals in paradir round the floor, or sat at tables tasting the tea or coffee.

In 1744 Horace Walpole remarked: 'Nobody goes anywher else – everybody goes there . . . You can't set your foot withou treading on a Prince of Wales or Duke of Cumberland. Th Company is universal; there is from his Grace of Grafton dow to children out of the Foundling Hospital – from my Lad Townshend to the Kitten [probably Kitty Fisher, the court san].' Ranelagh was so popular that at the height of th Gardens' season, in May, the roads leading there were ofte blocked by coaches. In May 1748 Horace Walpole complaine of a traffic jam which delayed his arrival by 36 minutes. In Jun of the same year Walpole was also at Vauxhall, where he sa 'a long procession of Prince Lobkowitz's footmen in very ric new liveries, the two last bearing torches; and after them th Prince himself, in a new sky-blue watered tabby coat, with gol buttonholes, and a magnificent gold waistcoat fringed, leadin Madame l'Ambassadrice de Venise in a green sack with straw hat, attended by my Lady Tyrawley . . .' They left in or of the Prince of Wales's barges, followed by 'another barg filled with violins and hautboys, and an open boat with drun and trumpets'. Getting across the river to Vauxhall could be troublesome in its different way as the road to Ranelagh. O one occasion in 1749 London Bridge was choked for thre hours – though once there the gardens were sufficient recon pense, as Smollett describes:

At nine o'clock, in a charming moonlight evening, we embarke at Ranelagh for Vauxhall, in a wherry, so light and slender,

that we looked like so many fairies sailing in a nut-shell. My
uncle, being apprehensive of catching cold upon the water,
went round in the coach, and my aunt would have accompanied
him, but he would not suffer me to go by water if she went by
land; and therefore she favoured us with her company, as she
perceived I had a curiosity to make this agreeable voyage . . .
The pleasure of this little excursion was, however, damped, by
my being sadly frightened at our landing; where there was a

A masquerade in the pleasure gardens
at Ranelagh, by George Cruikshank.
In the background is the Rotunda.

69

terrible confusion of wherries, and a crowd of people bawling, and swearing, and quarrelling; nay, a parcel of ugly-looking fellows came running into the water, and laid hold on our boat with great violence, to pull it ashore; nor would they quit their hold till my brother struck one of them over the head with his cane. But this flutter was fully recompensed by the pleasures of Vauxhall; which I no sooner entered than I was dazzled and confounded with the variety of beauties that rushed all at once upon my eye. (*Humphrey Clinker*, 1771)

While the ladies of literary tastes might attend a *salon*, the gentlemen resorted to their clubs. For men of wealth the London clubs provided congenial company and distraction from the cares of family and estate. They offered a home, always open, always comfortable, always convenient, where one could relax, play cards, talk gossip, read the newspapers, discuss politics or simply sleep the afternoon away. Clubs of a political nature first appeared in London soon after the Restoration, when they became private centres for the launching of new political manoeuvres and for influencing important politicians. Others were essentially forums for discussion, where free-thinkers could debate without restraint the problems in which their disbeliefs involved them. The most notorious free-thinking club of the eighteenth century was the Robin Hood Society, a name derived from the tavern in Butcher's Row where it convened on Monday evenings. Of the purely social clubs, the 'beefsteak' ones were among the earliest. One such was the Sublime Society of Beef Steaks, founded in 1735, which had close connections with Covent Garden Theatre. It was established by John Rich, a celebrated harlequin and machinist of the Theatre, and the members met in his room at two o'clock to partake of a hot steak dressed by Rich himself, washed down with a bottle of choice port. The members included George Lambert of the Theatre, Hogarth, Cibber, John Wilkes, the Earl of Sandwich, George Colman the playwright, Samuel Johnson and the Prince of Wales. In 1762 Lord Eglinton introduced Boswell into the Beefsteak Club, then conducted by 'the famous Mr Beard of Covent Garden Theatre'. Beard took Boswell 'up a great many steps to a handsome room above the theatre' where the club met, 'a society which has subsisted these thirty years'.

White's in St James's Street, the oldest of the modern clubs, began life as a chocolate house established shortly before the end of the seventeenth century. From the start it was a haunt of gentlemen of fashion, and developed as a notorious gaming-house. The advantages of exclusiveness as a way to keep out cheats, idle sightseers and other undesirables, no doubt influenced its metamorphosis into a club. White's flourished in a period when gambling became a craze. Richard Seymour's book of gaming rules, *The Compleat Gamester*, gave instructions for ombre, quadrille, quintille, picquet, basset, faro, chess, whist, all-fours, cribbage, put, loo, brag and billiards. The book reached a fifth edition by 1734, and a seventh by 1750. Bramston, writing in 1733, rhymed in his *Man of Trade*:

*Had I whole Counties, I to* White's *would go,*
*And set lands, woods, and rivers, at a throw.*

From the first, White's had a distinguished membership which included the Duke of Devonshire, the Earls of Cholmondeley, Chesterfield and Rockingham, and Major-General Churchill. Its reputation as an expensive gambling-house, where large stakes were the rule, was spread by hostile pamphleteers who called it a 'pit of destruction' and 'curse of the aristocracy'. Arthur Young, the famous agricultural writer, saw it in a different light, however. In his view the ideal landlord was not the penny-cautious, country-bound squire, but rather the reckless young rake who went to White's, gambled away all his money, and was forced to go back to the country to raise his rents in order to recoup the losses. Only good farming could

game of hazard, by Rowlandson, 792. The sporting pictures on the alls reflect the players' interests.

pay high rents, Young argued, and farmers whose rents were raised had no alternative but to farm more efficiently.

Gambling was also the main *raison d'être* of Boodle's and Crockford's, as well as of the new Whig club, Brooks's (formerly Almack's), where Horace Walpole remarked, 'a thousand meadows and cornfields are staked at every throw, and as many villages lost as in the earthquake that overwhelmed Herculaneum and Pompeii'. At Brooks's, Charles James Fox ran up debts of £140,000 by the time he was 24, and Lord Lauderdale spoke of as much as £5,000 being staked on a single card at faro, and of £70,000 won and lost in a single night.

There were many other clubs, principally of a social kind, providing facilities for dining and conversation. Such was one described by Edward Gibbon. It afforded, he said,

> a sight truly English. Twenty or thirty, perhaps, of the first men in the kingdom, in point of fashion and fortune, supping at little tables covered with a napkin, in the middle of a Coffee-room, upon a bit of cold meat, or a sandwich, and drinking a glass of punch. At present, we are full of Privy Counsellors and Lords of the Bedchamber; who, having jumped into the Ministry, make a very singular medley of their old principles and language, with their modern ones.

In the lower levels of London society the drinking club was commonplace. Such clubs met regularly at a particular inn, like the punch club which met at the public house kept by Francis Place's father: about 30 members convened every Monday evening at eight, and the proceedings terminated only 'when all the members were drunk'. Similarly, there were lottery clubs where members paid in a weekly sum towards buying lottery tickets, cutter clubs whose members took boats on the river, trade clubs for many different kinds of craftsmen, chair clubs where a different member took the chair on each occasion, clubs connected with particular sports, and 'spouting clubs' whose members had acquired a taste for public speaking. 'Cock and hen clubs' were doubtful assemblies of young men and prostitutes who met to drink and sing in disreputable alehouses. A sixpenny card club met at the Queen's Arms in St Paul's Churchyard, and the Cider Cellar in Maiden Lane was famous for its political debates and arguments.

Altogether more respectable and middle-class was the coffee house. Many were frequented by regulars, drawn together by a common occupation or business interest. Others catered for a more varied clientele of casual visitors and strangers. In *Amusements Serious and Comical*, Tom Brown offers this description:

A meeting at a pugilists' club, the members of which appear somewhat the worse for drink. The walls are adorned with pictures of Mendoza and Humphrys, noted boxers of the day, 1789.

'The Return from a Masquerade – a Morning Scene'. Note the leer on the bystander's face.

Every coffee-house is illuminated both without and within doors; without by a fine glass lantern, and within by a woman so light and splendid, you may see through her without the help of a prospective. At the bar the good man always places a charming Phillis or two, who invite you by their amorous glances into their smoky territories, to the loss of your sight. This is the place where several knights errant come to seat themselves at the same table, without knowing one another, and yet talk as familiarly together as if they had been of many years acquaintance: They have scarce looked about them, when a certain liquor as black as soot is handed to them, which being soppishly sum'd into their noses, eyes and ears, has the virtue to make them talk and prattle together of every thing but what they should do. Now they tell their several adventures by sea and land; how they conquered the giant, were overcome by the lady, and bought a pair of waxed boots at Northampton to go a wooing in. One was commending his wife, another his horse, and the third said he had the best smoked beef in Christendom. Some were discoursing of all sorts of government, Monarchical, Aristocratical, and Democratical; some about the choice of mayors, sheriffs and aldermen; and others of the transcendant virtues of vinegar, pepper and mustard. In short, I thought the whole room was a perfect resemblance of Dover-court, where all speak, but nobody heard or answer'd.

According to Professor Rudé, 'the coffee house, the newspaper, and even the novel, were the product of the City and of a commercial and middle-class, rather than an aristocratic, way of life'. The earliest coffee houses, he remarks, were largely concentrated within the square mile around the Royal Exchange. They survived a brief royal proscription in 1675 to flourish again as centres of political discussion and of business, and by 1739 London boasted well over 500 of them. In the coffee houses newspapers were read, events of the day discussed and affairs of commerce transacted. It was because of their importance as centres of news and commercial transactions that the more prestigious coffee houses developed as specialized financial institutions. The Stock Exchange, Baltic Exchange and Lloyds all originated in coffee houses. Others were used as regular meeting-places by bankers, physicians, artists and writers. The Cocoa Tree was a great Tory house, the St James's the resort of the Whigs. Will's Coffee House in Russell Street, Covent Garden, and Garraway's in the City were patronized by Addison and Steele, as well as by Swift and Gay; the Bedford Coffee House, also in Covent Garden, was the rendezvous of such famous figures as Pope, Sheridan, Garrick and Fielding. Anderton's in Fleet Street was beloved of free-

73

The view in Greenwich Park on Easter Monday, *c.* 1740.

masons and literary men, and Batson's in Cornhill was [a] famous meeting-place for physicians. Jonathan's in Exchang[e] Alley was essentially a stockjobbers' house, as was Baker's. '[I] have been taken for a Merchant upon the Exchange for abo[ut] these ten years, and sometimes pass for a Jew in the assembly [of] Stock Jobbers at Jonathan's', wrote Addison in the *Spectat[or]*. Young Man's, at Charing Cross, was fashionable among t[he] loungers and gamblers, and Old Man's, in the Tilt Yar[d,] Whitehall, was a rendezvous for army officers, but was lat[er] superseded by Slaughter's Coffee House in St Martin's Lan[e,] which later still was frequented by artists and sculpto[rs.] Searle's, at the corner of Lincoln's Inn Fields, was a lawyer['s] coffee house. The presence of famous personages, and t[he] lively discussions that arose, gave these coffee houses a wi[de] reputation and attracted many strangers. Thus it was to Wil[l's] that Nicholas Blundell directed his steps one evening when [he] was in London, and he noted in his diary that there he hea[rd] 'Mr Lawson talk of calculating Nativities'.

Thomas Telford, the celebrated canal engineer and brid[ge] builder, 'Pontifex Maximus' an admirer called him, resid[ed] for 21 years at the Salopian Coffee House, Charing Cros[s,] whenever he was in London. There he could engage addition[al] rooms for conference and to discuss business, and the Salopi[an] inevitably became a regular meeting place for his assistants a[nd] fellow engineers. Members of this growing profession dropp[ed] in to consult Telford or merely to hear of new contracts and t[he] latest moves in the transport world. Mr L. T. C. Rolt, in [his] book about Telford, tells us that he brought so much busin[ess] to the Salopian that when the premises changed hands Telfo[rd] was sold with them as a valuable item in the goodwill. Whe[n,] in 1821, Telford finally decided on a permanent residence a[nd] announced his departure, the unfortunate landlord, on[ly] recently in possession, exclaimed: 'What! leave the hous[e?] Why, Sir, I have just paid £750 for you.' The Institution [of] Civil Engineers, of which Telford was the first president, w[as] founded a few years before this, and met at Gilham's or t[he] Kendal Coffee House before acquiring its own premises [in] Buckingham Street, Strand.

Varying contemporary accounts of the character of coff[ee] houses have survived. Archenholtz found that:

> The politeness and activity with which you are served in
> coffee houses and taverns is astonishing, and seems a striking
> contrast to the national pride. But the waiters there depend on[ly]
> certain gratifications which amount to a considerable sum at t[he]
> year's end. Many of them indeed receive neither wages nor

board. In the principal taverns, the place of first waiter is purchased from the master of the house sometimes for two or three hundred pounds or more. In gaming houses where people of quality meet to play at games of hazard, it is common for the first waiter to pay five hundred pounds a year, and the second three for their places, because they produce a revenue of twelve or fifteen hundred pounds a year, and put the persons in a way, after a few years' service, of setting up a tavern on their own account. (*A View of the British Constitution and of the Manners and Customs of the People of England*)

Jonathan's Coffee House, when visited by Ned Ward, was frequented by the stockjobbers, who on this occasion were exhibiting great alarm at some unexpected turn in the markets: 'I saw a parcel of men at one table, consulting together with as much malice, horror, anger and despair in their looks, as if a new pestilence had sprung up in their families, and their wives had run away with their journeymen to avoid the infection.'

Newspapers were one of the attractions of the coffee houses, as they still remain in some continental countries. The first daily newspaper, the *Daily Courant*, appeared in 1702, followed by the *Evening Post* in 1706, and the famous weeklies, the *Tatler* and *Spectator*, in 1709 and 1711. A further spate of new journals made their appearance from 1725 onwards, and towards the end of the century those celebrated newspapers the *Morning Post* (1780), *The Times* (1785), and the Sunday *Observer* (1791) began publication. By the end of the eighteenth century the 5 newspapers and periodicals published in 1702 had swollen to a total of 278. The circulations by modern standards were very small – *The Times* sold only 5,000 copies in 1795 – partly because the stamp duty and the expense of current printing methods made newspapers fairly expensive. But since many copies went from hand to hand in coffee houses and clubs, the actual readership and influence of the London papers were far greater than the circulation figures suggest.

Skating in Hyde Park, 1785.

The visitor who sought convivial company when in town would probably spend much of his time in taverns, especially as he could eat there quite cheaply. Nicholas Blundell, when in London during December 1715, 'smoked a pipe in Vair Street', took a glass of Wine at the Wine Tavern in Holborn', and drank good March Beer' at the Cock and Hoop in the same area. He supped 'at a Cooks shop in New Turnstile', ate asparagus at Covent Garden', and oysters at Jefferson's Coffee House. Among the best known of the old taverns was The

Bear at the foot of London Bridge, Southwark, which had existed since 1463, and was not pulled down until 1761. The White Hart in Bishopsgate Without bore the date 1480 and survived until 1829. Others were the Boar's Head in Eastcheap, Pontack's in Abchurch Lane, the Pope's Head in Pope's Head Alley, and the Cock in Threadneedle Street, which was destroyed in 1851. Dr Johnson patronized the Mitre, the Devil, and the Crown and Anchor. But his favourite was the Turk's Head, where he had a regular chair and presided over 'The Club', a weekly dining society he founded with Reynolds in 1764. A writer of 1726 gives an amusing picture of a tailor ruminating on his tavern bill:

> Let me see – Bread and Beer – Tripe and Dressing – Hey Day!
> And Wine, and Welsh Rabbet – Here's the Devil to pay!
> And then, O' my Conscience, besides his long Bill,
> Out of ever'y poor Pint he has cabbaged a Gill.
> For all his fine Bows, and his Speeches, and Wheedle,
> I swear that a Vintner's as sharp as a needle.
>     The Vintner, in hearing, reply'd, 'tis your Pleasure
> 'Gainst another Man's Bill to run out beyond Measure.
> If we come to tax Reckonings, we all easily find
> Many Items and Items not at all to our Mind:
> There's your Silk, Twist, and Buckram; Materials and Making,
> And a Remnant – But pardon the Freedom I'm taking.
> Come, live and let live, without any repining:
> I pay for my Doublet; pay for your Lining.
> (in David Lewis, *Miscellaneous Poems by Several Hands*, 1726)

Steak-houses were also popular, like the well-known Dolly's in Paternoster Row in the City, which Boswell visited in December 1762. He thought a steak-house 'a most excellent place to dine at. You come in there to a warm, comfortable, large room, where a number of people are sitting at table. You take whatever place you find empty; call for what you like, which you get well and cleverly dressed. You may either chat or not as you like. Nobody minds you, and you pay very reasonably. My dinner (beef, bread and beer and waiter) was only a shilling.'

Many taverns were of doubtful reputation, the haunts of hucksters, pedlars, thieves and prostitutes. But others were highly respectable, like Dr Johnson's favourites the Turk's Head and the Mitre. The Doctor liked 'a pretty good tavern in Catherine-street in the Strand, where very good company met in an evening, and each man called for his own half-pint of wine, or gill, if he pleased; they were frugal men, and nobody

*Top* An eighteenth-century repast Lloyd's coffee house.

76

paid but for what he himself drank. The house furnished no supper; but a woman attended with mutton pies which anybody might purchase. I was introduced to this company by Cumming the Quaker, and used to go there sometimes when I drank wine.'

There were also formal dinners to which the well-connected might be invited. These were given frequently in the season by members of the aristocracy living in London, and by wealthy merchants and city businessmen. The London livery companies gave their annual feasts to which liverymen invited numbers of guests, and there was, of course, the annual Lord Mayor's Banquet. Although held amid the splendours of Guildhall, this great occasion was a somewhat less dignified affair than might be supposed. According to William Hickey, who attended Sir Watkin Lewis's Banquet on 9 November 1780, '...five minutes after the guests took their stations at the tables the dishes were entirely cleared of their contents, twenty hands seizing the same joint or bird and literally tearing it to pieces. A more determined scramble could not be, the roaring and noise was deafening and hideous, which increased as the liquor operated, bottles and glasses flying across from side to side without intermission ... This abominable and disgusting scene continued till near ten o'clock, when the Lord Mayor, sheriffs, nobility, etc, adjourned to the ball and card rooms and the dancing commenced.' But at this point Hickey's account comes to an end: 'completely exhausted' he went home to bed.

Between eating and drinking there were many strange and diverting sights to be seen, from the tombs in Westminster Abbey to the lunatics in Bedlam. Blundell saw 'five men and two women carted towards Tyburn there to be executed', and 'a woman whipped at ye cart's arse twice round Red Lion Square'. Of a different kind of interest were the 'looking glass as was in one piece 86 inches long and 44 inch wide valued at £130' which he was shown in 'ye New Exchange', the 'Wax Work and beasts in Fleet Street', the 'antilope and other beasts in Holborn', a 'show of monsters, *viz* a whelp with 8 legs and feet and one head etc', and 'ye moving images in Shanlow Street the first time they were showed'. Other curiosities on view in eighteenth-century London included a North American savage, an American elk, Bengal tigers, 'the real unicorn' (or rhinoceros), a dancing horse, Siamese twins, and a mermaid who was exhibited at Charing Cross. At St Bartholomew's Fair in August 1748, 'a wonderful and surprising satyr at the first house on the pavement from the end of Hosier

*bove* A tavern scene: the pretty bar-aid, by John Collet.

Lane' could be seen. In 1790 John Byng reported in his diary the arrival in London of Powell, the 'celebrated pedestrian', who for a wager walked to York and back within the time allowed, but who, said Byng, 'from a lack of roguery has this poor devil gained nothing by his powerful labours':

> This celebrated Pedestrian has won his wager – he arrived in York on Wednesday, between one and two o'clock – and on Saturday at St Paul's London; at twelve minutes after four – being an hour and forty-eight minutes within the time wagered for.
>
> He was met, at Highgate and Islington, by about 200 horsemen; and when he reached London, the crowd was immense. As soon as he had touched St Paul's Church-door, the mob gave him three huzzas. He then got into a hackney coach, and was driven to the Pheasant public-house at the back of Astleys Amphitheatre where he went to bed. Powell said he would undertake to walk one hundred miles this day, if any person would make it worth his trouble by a wager. (*Torrington Diaries*)

A banquet at the Mansion House.

Many of the human curiosities and strange animals mentioned above were a regular part of the annual fairs. The fairs also had merry-go-rounds and side shows, troops of actors and dancers, and stalls purveying food and drink. Roast pork was a particular speciality, and Edward Ward, who visited the Smithfield Fair early in the century, was moved to write:

> *No sooner had I pass'd the Gate,*
> *Where fetter'd Villains dread their Fate,*
> *And enter'd into Giltspur Street,*
> *But such a Nosegay did I meet,*
> *Arising from the Pig and Pork,*
> *Of greasy Cooks at sweating Work*
> *Enough to 've made a faithless Jew,*
> *Or freckly Scotch-man Keck or Spew.*
> *(Hudibras Redivivus, 1708)*

There were also the May Fair, the Lady Fair at Charlton, Whit Monday Fair at Greenwich, and Southwark Fair, but the most famous was St Bartholomew's Fair at Smithfield. Ward described the noise, 'the rumbling of drums, mixed with the intolerable squalling of catcalls and penny trumpets', the smell of singeing pigs and 'burnt crackling of over-roasted pork', and the sights – the mock finery of the actors 'strutting round their balconies in their tinsey robes and golden leather buskins, the rope dancers, and the buffoonery of the Merry Andrews'. There was also a most discordant instrumental concert, a youthful damsel performing a sword dance, and a

A panorama of the attractions at S Bartholomew's Fair, 1721.

oman who danced 'with glasses full of liquor on the backs of
er hands . . . without spilling'.

ore intellectual entertainment was provided by the theatre.
roductions ranged from opera, both Italian and English –
undell was diverted by 'ye English opera . . . called Diocles-
n' – to Shakespeare, and contemporary comedies by such
asters as Sheridan, Vanbrugh and Colman. John Gay's great
ccess, *The Beggar's Opera*, was first produced at the Lincoln's
n Fields Theatre in 1727, and its run of 62 nights was a
ntemporary record. After 1733, the year in which Covent
arden opened, the Covent Garden Theatre and the Theatre
oyal in Drury Lane were the most popular and fashionable of
e London playhouses, vying with the Italian Opera House
the Haymarket which relied on a more genteel patronage
sustain its exotic form of entertainment. Among the great
ayers of the age were Quin, Foote, Kemble, Mrs Cibber,
eg Woffington, Mrs Siddons, and above all, David Garrick.
arrick's revival of *The Beggar's Opera* in 1742 ran for 150
nsecutive nights, thus eclipsing the success of the first
oduction; Garrick himself earned the then substantial sum
£300 from it.

Southwark Fair, by Hogarth, 1733–4.

Seats were cheap, as little as a shilling in the gallery, two
illings in the pit and three shillings in a box off-stage in the
30s. Later in the eighteenth century, however, prices were
creased as actors' salaries and the other costs of production
l rose, and the theatres were rebuilt on a larger scale. John
yng greatly disliked the new Drury Lane Theatre. In *The
orrington Diaries*, he describes how in 1794 he went there to see
rs Siddons's 'highly wrought' performance 'in Catherine in
enry 8th', which was 'lost and sent to waste in this wild wide
eatre where close observation cannot be maintained, nor
uick applause received! Restore me', he went on, 'to the
arm close, observant, seats of Old Drury where I may
mfortably criticise and enjoy the delights of scenic fancy:
hese now are past! The nice discriminations, of the actor's
ce, and of the actor's feeling, are now all lost in the vast void
the new theatre of Drury Lane. Garrick – thou didst retire
the proper time – for wer't thou restored to the stage, in vain,
ould now thy finesse, thy bye play, thy whisper, thy aside,
d even thine eye, assist thee.'

A visit to the theatre in eighteenth-century London often
oduced as much excitement offstage as the performance on
age. Uproar among the patrons, and even brawling, were
ot uncommon, and might arise as easily from the appearance

Inside the theatre, 1813.

of some unpopular figure in the audience as from the quality the performance. Boswell described such an incident on December 1762, when he visited Covent Garden:

> at night I went to Covent Garden and saw *Love in a Village*, a new comic opera, for the first night. I liked it much, I saw it from the gallery, but I was first in the pit. Just before the overture began to be played, two Highland officers came in. The mob in the upper gallery roared out, 'No Scots! No Scots! Out with them!', hissed and pelted them with apples. My heart warmed to my countrymen, my Scotch blood boiled with indignation. I jumped up on to the benches, roared out, 'Damn you, you rascals!', hissed and was in the greatest rage. I am very sure at that time I should have been the most distinguished of heroes. I hated the English; I wished from my soul that the Union was broke and that we might give them another battle of Bannockburn. I went close to the officers and asked them of what regiment they were of. They told me Lord John Murray's and that they were just come from the Havana. 'And this,' said they, 'is the thanks that we got – to be hissed when we come home. If it was French, what could they do worse?' 'But,' said one, 'if I had a grup o yin or twa o the tamd rascals I sud let them ken what they're about.' The rudeness of the English vulgar is terrible. This indeed is the liberty which they have: the liberty of bullying and being abusive with their blackguard tongues. They soon gave over. I then went to the gallery and was really well entertained with the opera.

Sometimes there were unruly elements in the audience whom no performance could please. Productions to which the pit objected could easily be hissed off the stage. As Pope wrote in 1737,

> *There still remains to mortify a Wit*
> *The many-headed monster of the pit;*
> *A senseless, worthless, and unhonored crowd;*
> *Who, to disturb their betters mighty proud,*
> *Clatt'ring their sticks before ten lines are spoke,*
> *Call for the farce, the bear, or the black-joke.*

Charles Shadwell, writing 17 years earlier, had the same complaint:

> *There's not a vizzard sweating in the Gallery,*
> *But likes a smart intrigue, a rake, and raillery.*
> *And were we to consult our friends above,*
> *A pert and witty footman, 't is they love.*
> *And now and then such language as their own,*
> *As Damn the dog, you lie, and knock him down.*

To thwart this kind of behaviour theatre managers sometimes hired rival *claques*, and on one occasion, Horace Walpole
recalled, Mr Fleetwood, the master of Drury Lane Theatre,
'let into the pit great numbers of Bear-garden *bruisers* (that is
the term), to knock down everybody that hissed. The pit rallied
their forces, and drove them out . . . On a sudden the curtain
flew up, and discovered the whole stage filled with blackguards,
armed with bludgeons and clubs, to menace the audience. This
raised the greatest uproar . . . one of the actors advancing to
the front of the stage to make an apology for the manager, he
had scarce begun to say, "Mr Fleetwood" when your friend
with a most audible voice and dignity of anger, called out, "He
is an impudent rascal!" The whole pit huzzaed, and repeated
the words. Only think of my being a popular orator! But what
was still better, while my shadow of a person was dilating to the
consistence of a hero, one of the chief ringleaders of the riot,
coming under the box where I sat, and pulling off his hat, said,
"Mr W., what would you please to have us do next?" It is
impossible to describe to you the confusion into which this

'Theatrical Pleasures: Contending for
a Seat', 1821.

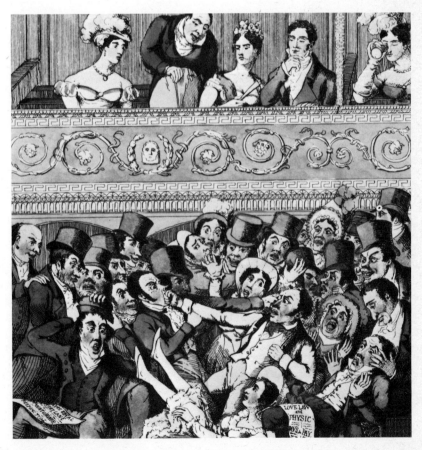

May Day dancing at Islington Spa, 1720.

apostrophe threw me. I sunk down into the box, and have never since ventured to set my foot into the playhouse.'

The post of 'box-keeper' at a London theatre was by no means a sinecure. At Covent Garden a Mr James Brandon who held this office was involved in a long series of violent incidents in the Theatre. On Boxing Day 1801, during a performance of *Richard III*, a drunken member of the audience threw a quart bottle at one of the actors. The ensuing disturbance was quelled only by Brandon's arrival with five guardsmen bearing fixed bayonets. A few years later Brandon had the task of sobering down the night's leading actor, George Cooke, who arrived drunk at a rehearsal. Fortunately Brandon's judicious application of coffee and wet towels enabled the performance to take place. When the new theatre at Covent Garden was opened on 18 September 1809 (the first theatre was burned down on 20 September 1808), an alarming situation developed. The opening night's performance of *Macbeth* and a musical farce called *The Quaker* was disrupted by rioters in the pit who threw hot coins about and stamped their feet, chanting in unison 'o.p.' (for 'old prices') as a protest against the new increased prices. In response the proprietor, John Kemble, produced a heavy squad of prizefighters headed by a well-known pugilist called 'Dutch Sam', and placed them under Brandon's leadership. The riots continued, however, and indeed went on for 66 days, supported by newspaper comment and broadsheets. In the end Kemble gave in to the demands of the o.p. rioters. The terms of his capitulation included:

1st. That the private boxes should, in number and in situation, be the same as they were in 1802, before Mr Kemble became Proprietor and Manager of the old Covent Garden Theatre.

2nd. That the price of admission to the pit should be reduced to 3s 6d but that the demand of 7s for the boxes should be allowed.

3rd. That an apology on the part of the Managers would be expected, and that Brandon, on account of his bad conduct, should forthwith receive his dismissal.

4th. That all prosecutions and actions on each side should be quashed.

Kemble was thus obliged to dismiss the theatre's box-keeper, though he was reinstated in the following year, and finally left the post in 1823 after almost 50 years' service.

And so after a beef-steak supper, a box at the theatre, a drink in a tavern – what? In the view of Boswell there could not be 'higher felicity on earth enjoyed by man than the participation

portrait of 'A Gentleman', by
Thomas Gainsborough.

of genuine reciprocal amorous affection with an amiable woman. There he has a full indulgence of all the delicate feelings and pleasures both of body and mind, while at the same time in this enchanting union he exults with a consciousness that he is the superior person. The dignity of his sex is kept up. These paradisical scenes of gallantry have exalted my ideas and refined my taste, so that I really cannot think of stooping so far as to make a most intimate companion of a groveling-minded, ill-bred, worthless creature, nor can my delicacy be pleased with the gross voluptousness of the stews.' Despite these high-minded sentiments, Boswell was not above seeking 'female sport' whenever it offered – albeit with a degree of caution. Having once suffered from venereal disease he did not wish to risk it again. So,

Went to a girl with whom I had an intrigue at Edinburgh, but my affection cooling, I had left her. I knew she was come up. I waited on her and tried to obtain my former favours, but in vain. She would by no means listen. I was really unhappy for want of women. I thought it hard to be in such a place without them. I picked up a girl in the Strand; went into a court with intention to enjoy her in amour. But she had none. I toyed with her. She wondered at my size, and said if I ever took a girl's maidenhead, I would make her squeak. I gave her a shilling, and had command enough of myself to go without touching her. I afterwards trembled at the danger I had escaped. I resolved to wait cheerfully till I got some safe girl or was liked by some woman of fashion. (*Boswell's London Journal, 1762–3*)

Boswell was probably not untypical of the young men of independent means who found in London's numbers and anonymity plenty of free play for licence, and what is commonly called experience. There were, too, many young girls who, attracted by the excitement of the supposed gay life of the capital, came fresh from the country to take up a career as some gentleman's mistress, or provide a new recruit to the brothels of Covent Garden.

Georgian London was not remarkable for its prudery or fastidiousness, and the rake and libertine had no difficulty in indulging his pleasures. It was an age of cynicism and sensuousness, and of excess, as the gross and licentious figures immortalized by Hogarth, Smollett and Fielding make clear. The capital, indeed, had many cruel and vicious aspects that were centred in the rookeries, slums and prisons, but also surfaced here and there in the politer districts of the West End. But this darker side was not the London of society, and will be dealt with separately in Chapter 5.

A busy dockside scene, showing a forest of masts with the Tower in the background. In the right foreground French wine has been unloaded and is being tasted by the vintners.

# 4 Commercial London

Oh, her lamps of a night! her rich goldsmiths, print-shops,
toy-shops, mercers, hardware-men, pastry-cooks, St Paul's
Churchyard, the Strand, Exeter Change, Charing Cross, with a
man upon a black horse! These are thy gods, O London!
Charles Lamb, *Letter to Thomas Manning*, 28 November 1800

Georgian London was not only the greatest city in the country, it was also the principal port and largest centre of commerce and manufacturing. As a port London had always dominated England's overseas trade. At the beginning of the Georgian period London handled about three-quarters of all English exports and four-fifths of the imports. While Bristol and Liverpool were growing in importance as centres for the West Indian, American and West African trades, and Whitehaven and Newcastle were the main ports for shipping coal, London played a major part in the trade with the New World and the East Indies, and predominated in the ancient commerce with Europe. Only the export of coal, the Irish trade and the ocean fishing industry were outside London's sphere of influence. Despite the rise of Bristol and Liverpool, London still imported most of the colonial produce, sugar, tobacco and rice, and tea and silks from the East Indies. Her strategic position opposite the major ports of western Europe also made London the obvious centre for the re-export business in colonial produce, a branch of trade which was expanding rapidly.

London was also the hub of the country's coasting trades. Hundreds of vessels were employed in bringing coal from Tyneside and Wearside; by 1750 about 650,000 tons a year were being shipped this way, a figure which accounted for about a sixth of the total national output. Adam Smith believed that the coal trade from Newcastle to London employed more shipping 'than all the carrying trades of England'. In addition to coal, grain, hops, fruit and fish were shipped to London from all round the east and south coasts. Cheese came round Wales and Land's End all the way from Cheshire, fish and tin came from Cornwall, nets and cordage from Dorset, and iron goods came up the Channel from the weald of Sussex.

Because of her leading role in both the foreign and coastal trades, London's shipping in the early eighteenth century was much the most extensive of any English port. In fact it far exceeded that of all the other ports put together. Defoe counted in the Pool of London and in the docks and reaches of Deptford and Blackwall 'above two thousand sail of all sorts, not reckoning barges, lighters or pleasure-boats, and yachts; but of vessels that really go to sea'. Between 1750 and 1795 the tonnage of ships from foreign and domestic ports entering the port of London more than doubled; by 1822 a total of 20,700 vessels were using the port. Nevertheless, as other ports expanded to serve the swelling industrial hinterlands of South Wales, Lancashire, Cumberland, Scotland and the north-east of England, so London's share of both the total shipping, and of

The Pool of London below London Bridge, by Samuel Atkins.

ipbuilding, declined. By 1770 the shipping, both English
d foreign, clearing the four next biggest ports, Whitehaven,
verpool, Newcastle and Bristol, totalled 345,126 tons, over a
ird as large again as London's tonnage of 212,876 tons. The
pital's commanding position in trade was also declining
ghtly: in 1770 London shipped out rather less than 70 per
nt of the country's exports, and received a little under 75
r cent of the imports.

The old shipyards at Blackwall, Millwall and Deptford
mained important, but there was a rapid expansion of

This painting of Blackwall Yard, by F. Holman, shows a number of vessels under construction. London was a great shipbuilding centre in the eighteenth century.

shipbuilding activity in the yards of the north and west, such as Glasgow, Leith, Newcastle and Sunderland. However, as London's volume of shipping and trade continued to grow congestion in the Thames became increasingly worse, causing serious delays in the loading and unloading of vessels in the Port of London. More docks were urgently needed to allow ships to discharge their cargoes directly to the quays and warehouses. The lightermen, naturally, opposed any change that would rob them of employment, and opposition also came from the Lord Mayor and Court of Aldermen of the City. But at length, in 1797, an Act was passed which established the West India Dock Company. The new West India Docks were opened in 1802, and were followed in the next few years by the London Docks, the East India Docks at Blackwall and the Surrey Commercial Docks on the south side of the river. The St Katharine Docks came in 1828. After this date there was no further major dock development until the mid-nineteenth century.

London's pre-eminence in trade and shipping made the capital the natural centre for insurance and finance. Marine insurance had its headquarters in Lloyd's Coffee House, and later moved to rooms at the Royal Exchange, where shipping news was readily available. Alongside marine insurance a fire insurance business grew up, and, in due course, life insurance. Fire offices increased rapidly in the early years of the eighteenth century, and by 1720 such well-known companies as the London Assurance, the Royal Exchange, the Westminster, the Hand-in-Hand and the Sun were already established. By 1850 there were 15 fire offices in London, including the Phoenix and the County. The companies maintained their own fire engines and identified the properties insured with them by a disting-

The Royal Exchange, an engraving by F. Bartolozzi after Chapman, 1788. Note the streams of wagons and coaches.

The Old East India Wharf at London Bridge, early in the Georgian period. A painting by Peter Monamy.

shing plaque fixed to the walls, some of which still survive on uildings of the period. They also developed a considerable olume of business outside London, and by the end of the ghteenth century they were insuring country houses, cotton ills and many other industrial and commercial undertakings the provinces. In 1785 the Royal Exchange Assurance issued policy on Richard Arkwright's steam-powered cotton mill, luing the mill and the engine-house together at £4,000. By e years 1816–20 the London Fire Offices had a total of £312m orth of property insured with them, out of a total of £388m sured for the whole of England and Wales. Some companies, e the Royal Exchange, the Albion and the Amicable, also veloped life insurance. The Equitable was the first company enter this field, as early as 1762, and by 1806 there were eight e offices in London. In 1816–20 the life insurance premiums the Royal Exchange Assurance totalled an average of 130,400 a year, compared with premiums of £64,000 paid r fire insurance.

Insurance, though important, was only one part of the nancial services provided by the capital. From about the iddle of the seventeenth century, London goldsmiths such as

The Bank of England, by Thomas
Malton, 1781.

Mocatta and Goldsmid had gradually developed regul
banking functions, receiving deposits, making loans, ar
transferring customers' funds by the use of cheques. The Ba
of England, established in 1694, made loans to the governmer
and in return had a monopoly of joint-stock banking in Englar
and Wales. In consequence, the other London banks (and lat
the English 'country' or provincial banks) had to operate o
the basis of capital provided by family firms and partnership
In 1725 there were 24 such banks in London, 42 in 1770, ar
by 1786 as many as 52. During the Georgian era the Londo
private banks started advancing loans, and discounting bills
exchange for London and provincial merchants. In additio
they acted as agents for the country banks, transferring fun
from areas where there was a surplus to those in which demar
exceeded the funds available, so playing a significant role
oiling the wheels of commerce, and facilitating the growth
the new industrial areas of the midlands and the north.

A degree of specialization grew up as some of the Londo
bankers concentrated on serving the commercial interests

A scene inside the Bank of England.

e City; these were located in and around Lombard Street,
nd included such well-known names as Martin's, and Vere,
lyn and Halifax. Other banks, mainly in Fleet Street and the
trand, the best-known being Hoare's and Child's, started to
ceive the rents of country landowners, arrange mortgages,
nd on bond, and generally act as the financial advisers of the
ealthy country gentry. Some of these bankers, like Richard
oare, eventually became country gentlemen themselves, and
entified themselves with the class they served. The bankers
eveloped a highly respectable, highly confidential and
onservative kind of image; and the appearance of their
emises tended to reinforce the sense of old-founded propriety,
illustrated in Dickens's account of Tellson's Bank in Fleet
reet (modelled on Hoare's), in the later years of the eighteenth
entury:

Tellson's Bank by Temple Bar was an old-fashioned place, even
in the year one thousand seven hundred and eighty. It was very
small, very dark, very ugly, very incommodious. It was an
old-fashioned place, moreover, in the moral attribute that the
partners in the House were proud of its smallness, proud of its
darkness, proud of its ugliness, proud of its incommodiousness.
They were even boastful of its eminence in those particulars,
and were fired by an express conviction that, if it were less
objectionable, it would be less respectable. This was no passive
belief, but an active weapon which they flashed at more
convenient places of business. Tellson's (they said) wanted no
elbow-room, Tellson's wanted no light, Tellson's wanted no
embellishment. Noakes and Co's might, or Snooks Brothers'
might; but Tellson's, thank Heaven!

Closely associated with London's import and export business was the growth of specialized markets and warehousing facilities, as well as industries concerned with processing imported raw materials, such as flour-milling, sugar refining, the manufacture of sulphuric acid and the bone-crushing and glue-making which were features of the Whitechapel and Stepney districts. England's sugar imports rose from less than half a million cwt per annum in the early years of the century to over $1\frac{1}{2}$ million cwt in 1770–71. Tobacco imports rose similarly from some 32 million lbs a year to nearly 50 million lbs. The rise of coffee and tea imports, however, was far more spectacular. Coffee imports, under 6,000 cwt a year at the beginning of the century reached over 40,000 cwt in 1770–71; and tea rose from a mere 70,000 lbs to almost 10 million lbs in the same period.

The growth of tea-drinking in England – which flourished despite the heavy import duties and the hostility of those who regarded the exotic beverage as demoralizing and enfeebling – made London Europe's main centre for the importing and blending of teas. Tea-drinking long remained a subject of controversy. John Wesley blamed his morning tea for 'some symptoms of a paralytic disorder', including a shaking of the hand, especially after breakfast. The pernicious effects of the beverage could be seen in many people in London, who had their 'nerves all unstrung, bodily strength quite decayed'. On 6 July 1746 Wesley proposed to his London Society that they should all renounce tea, and devote what they saved by this to helping the poor. Ten years later Jonas Hanway, the celebrated philanthropist and a founder of the Foundling Hospital, brought a variety of arguments to bear against tea, claiming that it obstructed industry and impoverished the nation on account of the quantity of silver bullion expended in purchasing it. In women it induced lassitude, low spirits and melancholy, and caused a decline in their beauty: 'The very chambermaids have lost their bloom by drinking tea.' Dr Johnson, the most 'hardened and shameless tea-drinker' of the age, was inclined to think that if tea had indeed such bad effects on the economy it should be prohibited. But he had no truck with Hanway's view on its effects on women: 'That there is less beauty in the present race of females than in those who entered the world with us, all of us are inclined to think, on whom Beauty has ceased to smile . . .' The debate continued, and even at the end of the Georgian period some people of conservative ideas were still regretting the widespread consumption of tea among the working classes, as being considerably less sustaining and ss health-giving than the beer it had replaced.

The East Indiamen that brought the tea cargoes from China riginally discharged them into warehouses near East India ouse, but the size of the vessels in the trade made it more onvenient for them to move to Blackwall where there was eeper water and less congestion. Following the success of the Vest India Dock Act, the East India Company in 1803 otained its own Act for the construction of a new dock to be sed exclusively by its vessels. The first ship, the *Admiral ardner*, entered the new dock on 4 August 1806, and the tea as unloaded into covered wagons to be conveyed direct to ie great tea warehouse, covering 5 acres, and with a main cade 700 feet long, which stood in Cutler Street, off Bishops- ite. Here, and at six other warehouses in Fenchurch Street, wry Street, Billiter Street and Crutched Friars near Tower ill, a staff of 4,000 warehousemen and 400 clerks prepared the a for market. To improve the road connecting the dock and ie warehouses, the East India Company subscribed £10,000 wards the building of two new thoroughfares, the East India ock Road and Commercial Road.

The import trades spawned a number of famous exchanges nd centres where the dealers in the various commodities met nd made their bargains. The one for tea was originally in the cinity of old East India House in Gracechurch Street, eadenhall Street and Coleman Street, and from 1834 in

The bustle of eighteenth-century trade: 'The Modern Tradesman, or the Glories of British Commerce': *When Europe shakes with War's alarms, 'Tis Trade can find Britannia Arms.*

Mincing Lane; the one for coal at the Coal Exchange was established in 1770 in Thames Street. Prior to this the coal market was held at the head of Billingsgate Dock, at a place called Room Land. Defoe, in *A Tour through England and Wales*, remarked on the great consumption of coal in London: 'Sometimes, especially in case of a war, or of contrary winds, a fleet of five hundred to seven hundred sail of ships, comes up the river at a time, yet they never want a market. The brokers, or buyers of these coals, are called crimps, for what reason, or original, is likewise a mystery peculiar to this trade; for these people are noted for giving such dark names to the several parts of their trade; so the vessels they load their ships with at Newcastle are called keels, and the ships that bring them, are called cats, and hags, or hag boats, and fly boats, and the like.'

Many of the marts grew up in coffee houses before moving into private premises. The merchants and sea-captains in the China and India trades gathered at the Jerusalem in Cornhill, just as those in the Baltic trade frequented the Virginia and Maryland Coffee House in Threadneedle Street, known from 1744 as the Virginia and Baltick. Marine insurance men, as we have seen, established themselves in Lloyds Coffee House in Pope's Head Alley, the merchant bankers concentrated at Garraway's in Cornhill and at Jonathan's and the Amsterdam by Temple Bar, while the origins of the Stock Exchange were to be found in the Stock Exchange Coffee House or Tavern in Sweeting's Alley.

Just as the commercial exchanges and the financial institutions of banking, insurance and the Stock Exchange grew up primarily to serve the needs of London's trade, so the great domestic market provided by London itself required the services of numerous produce markets. Defoe listed three fish markets at Billingsgate, Fishstreet Hill and Old Fishstreet, a cherry market at the Three Cranes, meal markets at Queenhithe, Hungerford, Ditchside and Whitecross Street, and markets for leather, hides and skins at Leadenhall and Wood's Close; the broadcloth market was at Blackwell Hall, and that for bays at Leadenhall. There were only two markets for corn, he remarked,

> but they are monsters for magnitude, and not to be matched in the world. These are Bear Key, and Queen Hithe. To the first comes all the vast quantity of corn that is brought into the city by sea, and here corn may be said not to be sold by cart loads, or horse loads, but by ship loads, and, except the corn chambers and magazines in Holland, when the fleets come in from Danzig and England, the whole world cannot equal the

quantity bought and sold here . . . The other, which I call a corn market too, is at Queen Hithe; but this market is chiefly, if not wholly, for malt . . . it must not be omitted that Queen Hithe is also a very great market for meal, as well as malt, and, perhaps, the greatest in England.

By the early years of the nineteenth century, when London ·asted over a million inhabitants, the produce markets had ·rforce expanded and multiplied. Covent Garden had now to ·ndle the produce of the 15,000 acres of market gardens that ·re cultivated within 10 miles of the metropolis, as well as ·e more distant gardens and orchards of Kent, Essex and ·dfordshire; and Billingsgate still attempted to cope with the ·panded supply of fish, as Newgate and Farringdon did for

Hungerford Market, 1825, an important centre for meat. The market was established by Sir Edward Hungerford in the seventeenth century, and stood near York Buildings in the Strand.

95

dead meat. Smithfield remained the principal market for li
cattle and sheep, dealing in 1828 with 153,000 cattle, and ov
$1\frac{1}{2}$ million sheep. It was also a centre for the trade in horses,
Ned Ward recalls in *The London Spy*:

> What are those eagle-looked fellows in their narrow brimmed
> white beavers, jockey coats, a spur in one heel, and bended
> sticks in their hands, that are so busily peeping into every
> horse's mouth? . . . Those blades, says my friend, are a subtle
> sort of Smithfield foxes, called horse coursers, who swear every
> morning by the bridle that they will not, from any man, suffer
> a knavish trick, or ever do an honest one. They are a sort of
> English Jews, that never deal with any man but they cheat hir
> and have a rare faculty of swearing a man out of his senses,
> lying him out of his reason, and cozening him out of his money
> if they have a horse to sell that is stone blind, they'll call a
> hundred Gods to witness that he can see as well as you can. If
> he be downright lame, they will use all the asseverations that t
> Devil can assist them with, that it is nothing but a spring halt;
> and if he be twenty years old, they'll swear he comes but seven
> next grass, if they find the buyer has not judgement enough to
> discover the contrary.

London was not only a great market for foodstuffs but al
an important centre for manufactures, and particular
luxury goods. Country gentlefolk ordered from London t
items they could not obtain in their local market town – fi
cloths, fashionable articles of dress, books, furniture, toil
requisites, medical preparations and the rarer kinds of tab
delicacies. Christiana Spencer of Cannon Hall, Yorkshir
wrote to her father in London for a bottle of salad oil, 'a Bar
of Sweet Soap', anchovies, capers, pickles, tea and coffe
Similarly, in 1739, Henry Purefoy of Shalstone in Buckinghan
shire ordered by post the following items from a Mr Bud
'stationer near the Pump in Chancery Lane' (postmen ha
something to complain about in those days):

> 2 quarts of the best ink in a stone bottle tied down & sealed on
> ye cork.
> 12 large sized wooden Pencils.
> Four diary books in quarto printed according to the paper sen
> & bound in smooth black calf and to be double leathered or
> made stronger on the edge of the lids next the binding, because
> the lids always wear out & crack next the binding.
> Some pieces or slips of parchment.
> Three quarts of sand, to sand writing, done up in strong paper
> so as not to spill.
> 2 dozen quire of small brown paper.
> 2 dozen quire of issue paper.

Two dozen quire of cut paper at 8d a quire.
12 sticks of superfine red sealing wax.
12 quire of largish sized gilt paper.
2 quire of blue paper.
Half an hundred of the best Dutch pens.

Pray send these things in 3 weeks' time at farthest by Mr Eagles the Buckingham carrier . . . & give the carrier a charge they come to no wet. I suppose you had as good send the things to the carrier on Monday night by reason they set out so early on Tuesday morning, & let me have a letter by the post with your bill of what they come to, that I may send to the carrier for them & order you payment.

rom a tailor he ordered in 1736 a coat and breeches with

buttons & trimming of the same colour, the coat to be lined with a shagreen silk & to be half trimmed & but one pair of breeches which I desire may be made the same size as ye breeches sent with pockets on each side, but no flap to the codpiece. The wastcoat to be a very good unwatered tabby the same green to ye pattern trimmed with silver buttons & a silver lace about the breadth of the gold lace I had last year on my wastcoat, & to have pockets to it.

Other miscellaneous orders made at various times included gallons of brandy, a hogshead (small barrel) of port wine, ılf a hogshead of white mountain wine, 3 gallons of the best ck, 4 lbs of grass seed, 1 quart of peas, and 'three bottles of e Tincture for preserving the Teeth and two Tooth Brushes om Mr Greenoughs near St Sepulchre's Church, on Snowhill'. is mother, Mrs Purefoy, also had a variety of things sent down Buckinghamshire by the carrier's wagon. These included 'a ry good whale bone hoop petticoat of the newest fashion', and wo Caroline hats of a fashionable size for the servants. Let em be so good as to be serviceable. The bignesse of the head the outside of the crown of the hats is twenty three inches und each; let each of them be laced with a gold lace of an ch & half a quarter of an inch wide & to have gold loops and ld buttons.'

The orders were not always very faithfully executed, and ail order business then, as now, had its disadvantages. Mrs urefoy had to have a Mr Potts reminded that 'every now & en his people send my son the *Whitehall* instead of the *London vening Post*, & to sent it right for ye future.' And Henry Pure-y was annoyed over some spectacles he sent to London for pair. In 1748 he had to write to a 'Mr Joseph Hurt at the rchimedes & 3 golden Spectacles near Ave Mary Lane in udgate Street' as follows:

You have made an ugly mistake in relation to my glasses, for I
sent to you for six concave glasses number six for my spectacles,
to repair ye same when they chance to break, & you have sent
me six glasses in horn cases which are of no use to me for I have
damaged one of my eyes already by using such as these are, &
now use only those that are put in spectacles; so must desire
you to change these six for as many concave glasses No 6
(without any cover or spectacles to them) as come to 12s which
my friend Mr Land paid you for these I send you. When I have
ye glasses I will put them into ye spectacles myself. I desire you
will send them by ye Buckingham carrier . . . You yourself fitted
up several spectacles of concave glasses No 6 for me in 1743 at
my Lodgings in little Lincoln's Inn Fields, so wonder you should
make this mistake . . . (G Eland, ed., *Purefoy Letters, 1735–53*)

To supply this country trade, as well as to meet the needs of
London residents, the principal manufacturers established
warehouses and depots in the capital, as did, for example,
Josiah Wedgwood, the leading midland pottery manufacturer,
and Wills of Bristol, the expanding tobacco firm. Though many
such manufacturers had an eye on London's market for
expensive luxury goods, they catered also, and often chiefly,
for the growing markets offered by the middle and working
classes. Wedgwood, despite the fame of his Jasper ware, in fact
made most of his money out of the ordinary pottery sold in
quantity to housewives of moderate means. The relatively high
level of wages in London served both to broaden the range of
goods sold in working-class districts, and to drive out of the
capital those trades which, like hosiery and shoemaking,
depended on low labour costs.

Other factors which encouraged the growth of manufacturing outside London included access to raw materials, fuel and
water power, and the introduction of technical advances
which, for example, made Lancashire the centre of cotton
production, Yorkshire that of woollens, and the Black Country
that of light engineering, glass, brass and copper goods. In
addition, the limited but still significant hold that the London
livery companies maintained on their various trades was often
sufficient to deter those industrialists who wished to develop
new processes and products without interference. Furthermore
many London workmen such as the Spitalfields silk-weavers
were well-known for their hostility to new machines and novel
methods of manufacture; a hostility often demonstrated in
machine-breaking riots. So, in the interest of maintaining peace
within the trade, the livery companies adopted a reactionary
attitude towards innovations. The London Weavers' Company,

r instance, paid rewards to informers who assisted in the
rosecution of those weavers found to be making prohibited
alicos and chintzes; and immigrant weavers who had taken
p the trade without becoming members of the Company
ere liable to be harried by the Company's officers. True, the
Veavers' Company abandoned its 'search of the trade' in
736, and completely ignored offences committed by the more
rosperous and influential masters, such as taking in too many
pprentices and operating an excessive number of looms;
evertheless, the London crafts acquired a reputation for
onservatism which added to the other forces encouraging the
se of industry outside the city.

The trades which remained and developed in London were
rgely those connected with its shipping and import-export
usiness, such as shipbuilding and bargebuilding, cooperage,
ıgar-refining, and the like, or those catering for the needs of
ıe mass of consumers located in and around the capital.
rewing, distilling, flour-milling, leather-tanning and manu-
cturing were closely connected with the day-to-day demands
London's working classes. Other luxury trades, such as
ırniture-making, the manufacturing of jewellery, clock- and
atch-making, cutlery, surgical instruments, paper-making,
rinting, candle-making, saddlery, silk-weaving, mantua-
aking, millinery and a large section of the tailoring trade
ere more largely concerned with the custom of the aristocracy
ıd the wealthy middle classes.

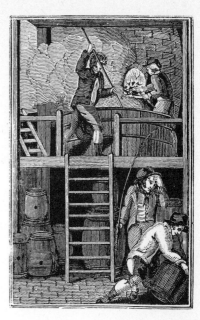

The brewer, from *The Book of English Trades*, 1823.

The extent to which London was a manufacturing centre
ıs not always been fully realized. The capital is more usually
ought of as the home of government and the professions,
articularly as the law courts were centralized at Westminster
all, and the Inns of Court served as nurseries for young
torneys. London became the natural resort of those seeking
xpert legal advice and was the scene of most important
igation. In addition, the growth of the London teaching
ospitals made it the centre – in England at least, if not in
cotland – for medicine and the training of doctors and
ırgeons. London was also the country's major city for the
rovision of mercantile, banking and insurance services. But
ıe growth of London's population, and the annual migration
the capital of thousands of country gentry, provincial
ıwnsmen and foreign visitors, also made it the major centre
ır manufactured goods of all descriptions. Certain trades, it is
ue, had deserted the capital in search of cheaper, and perhaps
ore docile, labour – silk-weaving to country towns like
Iacclesfield and Congleton, framework-knitting to Notting-

The linen draper, from *The Book of English Trades*, 1823.

ham and Leicester and their surrounding villages, and shoemaking to Northampton – but nevertheless, at the opening of
the Georgian era, something like one out of every four Londoners still earned his livelihood from manufacturing. Even
in 1861, when the industrial revolution had transformed the
midlands and the north, manufacturing industries still employed more than one in seven of London's occupied population, as compared with a proportion of nearly one in four
engaged in the professions and the service industries.

Within London there was a marked tendency towards local
specialization. Of the bulky consumer trades catering primarily
for the local population, brewing, distilling and vinegar-
making were for the most part established at some distance
from the centre. By 1786, the rise of the great London breweries,
each with an annual output of anything from 10,000 to 150,000
barrels of strong beer, had killed off the small licensed victual-
ler who used to brew his own beer. It was an industry of
considerable scale: in 1786 the London breweries produced a
total of nearly 5 million barrels of porter, $1\frac{1}{2}$ million barrels of
small beer and more than half a million barrels of table beer.
In 1814 the largest of them, Barclay Perkins, was established
in Southwark; Truman, Hanbury & Buxton had their headquarters in Brick Lane, Spitalfields; Meux was in the Tottenham
Court Road; Samuel Whitbread in Chiswell Street, St Luke's;
Watney's was to be found in Pimlico, and Charrington's in
Mile End Road.

The south bank of the Thames was the home of a variety of
heavy, bulky and noxious trades. Southwark, in particular, was
a centre for odorous tanneries and leather-dressing establish-
ments (as also was Bermondsey), as well as housing soap- and
candle-makers. With Lambeth, Southwark was also the home
of London's engineering businesses. John Rennie, who produced the designs for Southwark, Waterloo and London
bridges, had his business there, as had Joseph Bramah, the
fertile inventor of locks, the water closet and the beer engine.
Among Bramah's employees was the famous Henry Maudslay,
inventor of the hydraulic press, who eventually set up on his
own to manufacture the machine tools and marine engines
he designed. Coade Stone, a composition for which the formula
has now been lost, was manufactured on the south bank to
serve as decorations for Georgian houses and to meet the needs
of the pottery trade; it was later used for the lions which guarded
the entrance to Waterloo Station. Further west the River
Wandle, like other London rivers, was a hive of mills, notably
for calico-printing, bleaching, flour-milling and snuff manu-

facture. From 1803 the horse-drawn wagons on the Surrey Iron Railway connected Wandsworth with the Croydon area to the south. Lambeth was also favoured by potteries and timber yards; and, together with the parishes eastwards along the river, housed the Thames fishermen and those of mysterious waterside occupations.

North of the Thames, silk-weaving, early established in Whitechapel and Shoreditch, had spread by the Georgian period to Stepney and Spitalfields, and thence to Bethnal Green, Moorfields and Mile End. The arrival of Huguenot silk-weavers after the anti-Protestant disturbances in France towards the end of the seventeenth century, and especially after the Revocation of the Edict of Nantes in 1685, was a factor in the spread of the industry, and led to complaints to the Weavers' Company of excessive numbers of strangers in the trade, and that 'many foreign members now employ more French than English'. The trade became most closely associated with the Spitalfields district, where the workshops in the weavers' houses could be distinguished by their long attic

Coach-makers at work, eighteenth century. The trade was concentrated in Long Acre.

windows. The numbers of silk-weavers declined sharply from the middle 1820s when their wages ceased to be regulated and their trade was no longer completely protected. Silk-weaving firms using power-looms spread in Cheshire, Lancashire, Derbyshire and the West Country, but in London, where the industry failed to move with the times, the larger manufacturers laid off their looms and gave more of their business to the new power-loom factories in the provinces. As silk-weaving declined the tailoring industry expanded. In the West End it catered for the high-class bespoke trade of the wealthy, while in districts like Stepney, Bethnal Green and Whitechapel, poor immigrant Jews, in their homes and small workshops, ran up cheap shirts and dresses by the dozen for miserably low wages.

The West End, with the varied demand arising from its well-to-do residents, attracted poulterers (who were not above selling illegally-acquired game), cheesemongers, wine merchants, gunsmiths, high-class tailors, shoemakers, dressmakers and milliners, clock-makers and cabinet-makers. But many of the goods required in the West End came from further afield. Milk was retailed from the town dairies concentrated round Islington. Pottery came from Chelsea, Lambeth and Bow. Coaches were made to order by the specialist coach-builders of Long Acre. Furniture businesses had their workshops in Tottenham Court Road and in Curtain Road in the east. Pianos could be obtained in Soho, and the name of Hatton Garden became synonymous with jewellery. Clerkenwell was the leading centre for clocks, watches and scientific instruments. Printers established themselves in Holborn, Finsbury, the City and Southwark, while booksellers and card-makers opened their shops in the commercial district growing up around the Strand. Large printing firms first emerged in the early years of the nineteenth century, some of the more prominent being William Clowes, Waterlows, and Eyre & Spottiswoode. The area around Fleet Street and Ludgate Circus became the centre of newspaper offices. In 1814 John Walter, proprietor of *The Times*, installed the first steam-driven presses in Printing House Square, an important step towards the eventual appearance of the cheap, mass-circulation newspaper. In addition, many other crafts, to escape from the regulations of the livery companies, gilds and the City's Common Council, concentrated in a variety of areas, mainly in the East End, beyond the jurisdiction of these bodies; and each district possessed its characteristic groups of textile, woodworking, metalworking and other tradesmen.

A dairyman's shop in Golden Lane the City, towards the end of the Georgian era.

The growth of London's industrial districts, and the expansion of the population engaged in commerce, crafts and the service occupations, reinforced the demands for social improvement, advances in public health conditions, and the other requirements of a civilized society, while at the same time emphasizing the need for reform of the capital's government. At the centre of the problem of governmental reform in London stood the City Corporation. Its authority was extensive, stretching from Temple Bar in the west to the Tower in the east; its monopoly over markets had a radius of 7 miles; its levy on coal a radius of 12 miles; and it controlled the Thames from as far upstream as Staines right down to its confluence with the Medway by the Isle of Sheppey – a distance of 80 miles. The growth of London's trade and its urgent needs for new docks, enlarged markets, and new thoroughfares were largely ignored by the City. Indeed, the City's system of government, developed over the centuries, was so immensely complex that it defied simple description. Of the 17 courts, the four main ones, presided over by the Lord Mayor, had differing functions and constitutions. Since the seventeenth century the Court of Wardmote, open to the ratepayers of each ward, had been in decline, and there ensued a long period of rivalry and dispute between the three other principal courts. Gradually, towards the end of the seventeenth century, the Court of Common Council developed as the City's supreme executive, and came to overshadow the Court of Aldermen and the Court of Common Hall. Of these three, the Court of Common Council was the most broadly based, being composed of the Lord Mayor, the 25 other Aldermen and some 210 Councilmen elected annually by the freemen ratepayers; the Court of Aldermen consisted of the Lord Mayor and the 25 other Aldermen, who were elected for life, and were frequently aristocratic, non-resident, and wealthy businessmen; and the Court of Common Hall, which after 1725 was open only to freemen of the City's livery companies, although it still had the right to elect the Lord Mayor, the two Sheriffs of London and Middlesex, and the City's four Members of Parliament. The Court of Common Council, which was most closely associated with the ordinary residents of the City, gradually assumed a larger responsibility for legislation and administration, and its role continued to grow in the nineteenth century. However, the City remained extremely jealous of its rights and privileges, and was the only great municipal corporation to survive intact the demand for local government reform which culminated in the Municipal Corporations Act of 1835.

The City's 89 companies and gilds, which played a prominent part in the government of the City, had long been exclusive
and wealthy oligarchies. Entry to them was restricted by birth,
purchase and costly apprenticeship, and was beyond the
means of ordinary craftsmen. By the Georgian period the
companies had largely ceased to have any active connection
with the crafts they had originally controlled. Some, like the
Weavers' Company, still attempted in the first half of the
eighteenth century to regulate entry to the craft, collect fees,
and supervise apprenticeship and conditions of work; it also
sought to intervene in the numerous disputes which revolved
round the Spitalfields silk-weavers. Others had dropped all
but a pretence of exercising ancient functions, and had evolved
into close societies of wealthy merchants and city figures.
Much of their time was devoted to maintaining their meeting
hall, perpetuating traditional ceremonies, and pursuing
charitable functions.

Beyond the bounds of the City, authority for the administration of the police and the care of the poor was held by the
Justices of Middlesex and Surrey, as in other counties. In
Middlesex and Westminster many of the justices were not
well-to-do gentry but middle-rank professional men or tradesmen. Perhaps this contributed to the scandal of the 'trading
justice', where a justice made the office pay its way by charging
fees for the services rendered, and by deliberately promoting
court business so as to maximize the court's income. From time
to time a vigorous and reforming Chairman of Quarter Sessions
would get corrupt justices removed from the bench: such a one
was Sir John Hawkins who chaired the Middlesex Bench from
1765 to 1780. Others, less public-spirited, filled the county
offices with their cronies and relations. In such circumstances
corruption abounded, as happened in Middlesex under the
régime of William Mainwaring. He followed Hawkins as
Chairman, and presided over Quarter Sessions for 35 years of
graft and bribery until 1816.

At the parochial level offices were in the hands of the vestries.
Their powers varied considerably. Some vestries, as in the City,
had control of only very minor matters. Others exercised
extensive powers over highways, poor relief, sanitation and the
levying of rates, as in Marylebone and St Pancras. The great
majority of the vestries were 'open' for all or certain of their
functions: that is to say, the ratepayers were allowed to attend
and vote at the meetings. Partly in order to cope with increased
responsibilities and obtain greater administrative efficiency,
'close' or 'select' vestries, limited to a small group of leading

*Right* Buying fish in a London market
1822.

*Below* The interior of the hall of the
Auction Mart, Bartholomew Lane
*c.* 1808–10.

inhabitants, became the rule in a number of parishes. By the end of the eighteenth century about a quarter of the 200 metropolitan parishes were administered in this way. Marylebone, after gaining new powers in 1756, became a select vestry in 1768. The parish of St Pancras, which for long was ruled by an open vestry, grew in population from a few hundred to nearly 32,000 in the last quarter of the eighteenth century, and by 1821 had 72,000 inhabitants. The consequent inefficiency and chaos in the parish's affairs resulted in the assumption of control by a select vestry in 1819, following a long campaign led by one of the leading landowners. In some parishes the vestry fell under the sway of a local boss, rather after the style of later American city bosses. In Bethnal Green, for instance, the open vestry was dominated for many years by Joseph Merceron, the owner of many of the parish's beer shops. Merceron maintained his popularity by keeping the beer flowing throughout the night hours, and by staging bullock hunts and Sunday dog-fights. In 1818 justice eventually caught up with him, and he was sentenced to 18 months' imprisonment for the fradulent conversion of thousands of pounds of the parish funds. Nonetheless, his popularity and influence were such that after serving his sentence he succeeded in returning to power.

As the Georgian era continued, the need to provide new local services was often met by the creation of new bodies entirely separate from the parochial authorities. Turnpike trusts, for example, were established to supervise major thoroughfares, and improvement commissions were set up to look after such matters as street paving, lighting and cleansing. By the early years of the nineteenth century there were as many as 50 turnpike trusts in London, and some parishes had sprouted a bewildering maze of improvement commissions: St Pancras, for example, eventually boasted as many as 18 separate paving trusts. For the whole of London there were 8 Metropolitan Commissions of Sewers, bodies not noted for their efficiency: until 1817 the Westminster Commission had even neglected to make a plan of its own drains. The reform of this administrative jungle was delayed until the 1820s. A short time before, the two Sturges Bourne Acts, of 1817 and 1819, had amended the powers of open vestries and allowed a parish to elect a committee for the management of poor relief but with little long-term effect. In 1826, however, amalgamation of the turnpike trusts north of the Thames led to the provision of better roads and reduced tolls. Then, in 1829 came a major reform with the establishment of the Metropolitan Police – 'the one great reform of the first half of the nineteenth century in which London showed the way for the rest of the country', as Francis Sheppard remarks. Gone at last were the ancient constables and watchmen – too often elderly, corrupt and inefficient – and with them went Henry Fielding's Bow Street Runners, which had become little more than a 'disreputable private detective agency'.

But Peel's important measure was only achieved because he by-passed the Corporation of the City, still jealous of its privileges and resistant to ideas of reform. The physical growth of London was closely bound up with the general economic expansion and population increase which characterized the country in the Georgian age. At the opening of the period, in

Officers of the watch, armed with lantern and staves, question a drunk on his way home through the streets of London. Eighteenth century.

he 1720s and 30s, London was already a monster city by contemporary standards, and it grew still further until its sheer size and complexity aggravated both the need for, and the difficulty of, achieving governmental reform. Because of the rapidity of its growth, and the entrenched character of its institutions and interests, London exemplified more acutely than any other English city the fearful problems which arose when a long-accumulated labyrinth of rival agencies of government was faced with the pressures created by the explosion of population. Such problems arose more rapidly than they could be solved, and indeed it was many years before the need to find new and radical remedies was fully appreciated. At the end of the Georgian era, some hundred years later, only a modest beginning had been made towards bringing traditional customs and time-hallowed machinery into line with the demands of the new urban civilization.

A horse sale at Hopkins's Repository, Barbican, from a drawing by Rowlandson.

Scene inside the Fleet Prison, as
drawn by Hogarth in *A Rake's Progress*.
Published 1735.

# 5 The Darker Side of London

'Hell is a city much like London.'
Shelley, 'Peter Bell the Third'

Georgian London was a city of contrasts, of fashionable square
rustic walks, elegant society and soundly based, prudentl
conducted business-houses; but it was also a city of squali
slums, fetid back alleys, daring thieves, hideous beggars an
diseased prostitutes, fraudulent tradesmen and bold confidenc
tricksters. In the eighteenth century there was evidence tha
London's criminal class was not only growing but was als
becoming more adventurous. Highwaymen were reported a
leaving the dark thickets of Hounslow Heath to appea
brazenly in the very heart of the capital, and coach passenge
were robbed even in High Holborn and Pall Mall. In the earl
1750s Henry Fielding, novelist and senior Bow Street magis
trate, initiated a new drive against crime, and a few years late
it was reported, rather too optimistically it appears, that th
criminal forces were in retreat, with robbery, house-breakin
and shoplifting all checked, and many of the malefacto
brought to justice.

In fact, as Professor Rudé has pointed out, the volume
crime continued to rise. In 1768, 613 people were tried f
murder, burglary, robbery and theft. Over half of these wer
convicted, and 47 were sentenced to death. Highway robberi
were still carried out in the most respectable parts of the capita
Sir Francis Holbourne and his sisters were robbed in the
coach by a mounted highwayman in St James's Square i
1773, and in the 1780s the Prince of Wales and the Duke
York were robbed in Hill Street, Berkeley Square, in broa
daylight. In 1743, William Shenstone wrote in a letter how

> the pickpockets, formerly content with mere filching, make no
> scruple to knock people down with bludgeons in Fleet Street ar
> the Strand, and that at no later hour than eight o'clock at nigh
> but in the Piazza, Covent Garden, they come in large bodies,
> armed with couteaus, and attack whole parties, so that the
> danger of coming out of the play-houses is of some weight in th
> opposite scale, when I am disposed to go to them oftener than
> ought.

By 1794 the number of malefactors brought to trial at th
Old Bailey was over twice as great as in the 1760s; 493 perso
were convicted that year, and 68 of them sentenced to execu
tion. Patrick Colquhoun estimated that by the end of th
century London's criminal class was well over 100,000 stron
though half of this number consisted of 'lewd and immora
women'. The numbers of swindlers, thieves, pilferers, receive
of stolen goods, coiners, burglars and highway robbers ra
into thousands.

A great deal of petty crime, such as shoplifting and stre

pilfering, was carried out by gangs of juveniles. Oliver Twist and his fellow-graduates of Fagin's school had many counterparts in the eighteenth century. The stealing of handkerchiefs, scarves, purses and watches was undertaken by both children and adults. Dr Johnson once had his handkerchief taken by 'a sturdy thief' in Grosvenor Square, but to the thief's surprise the burly Doctor seized him by the collar, shook him violently and smacked him so hard in the face that the thief staggered off the pavement. Confidence tricksters, too, abounded and were not afraid of practising their subtle arts on the greatest in the land. Lord Chancellor Northington, walking one afternoon in Parliament Street, picked up a ring which was immediately claimed by a professional ring-dropper. This gentleman expressed the warmest gratitude for the restoration of his ring and insisted on the Lord Chancellor's accompanying him to an adjoining coffee house, there to crack a bottle in celebration. At the coffee house, in a private room, they were joined by the ring-dropper's confederates, who abandoned their original plan of engaging their quarry in a game of hazard to be played with loaded dice and decided instead to 'pick the old flat's pocket at once'.

The extent of crime in the metropolis was blamed, in part, on the growth of the capital's Irish population, 'a set of fellows made desperate by their crimes, and whose stay in Ireland being no longer safe, come to London to perpetrate their outrages, and it may be justly asserted that most of the robberies, and the murders consequent upon them, have been committed by these outcasts from Ireland . . . That London is the asylum of these rogues and vagabonds as well Irish as English who are driven by their rogueries to seek shelter and concealment is a truth beyond dispute . . .' Many of the poor Irish congregated in the common lodging houses of the St Giles district, where beds could be obtained for 2d a night and gin at a penny a quarter-pint. Poverty, ignorance, unemployment and destitution drove some of these immigrants to crime, and the Irish as a whole gained a bad reputation for drinking and quarrelling. In 1817 the Irish of St Giles were said to be 'a description of people that if they are in labour and they come home on the Saturday night with their wages, those wages are spent on the Saturday night or Sunday morning and then they shuffle on the rest of the week with their herrings or potatoes . . .' According to another contemporary, 'early on the Sunday morning you will see Irishmen quite drunk and fighting with their shelelas . . . at times three or four hundred . . .'

Another immigrant group, the Jews of east London, mostly

uneducated and very poor, were generally believed to live by their wits and to be heavily engaged in the passing of counterfeit coins and dealing in stolen goods. According to Colquhoun they were 'educated in idleness from their earliest infancy . . . they acquire every debauched and vicious principle which can fit them for the most complicated arts of fraud and deception . . . from the orange boy and the retailer of seals, razors, glass and other wares in the public streets, to the shopkeeper, dealer in wearing apparel or in silver and gold, the same principles of conduct too generally prevail.' There was no doubt that some poor Jews entered into criminal activities, though often this was for lack of any other employment. The truth, however, was that the typical Londoner was suspicious of all foreigners, and was inclined to ascribe to them all the long-established evils of the capital's underworld. It was not merely the Jews who bore the brunt of the general hostility; it extended to all those whose speech or appearance proclaimed them a stranger.

As Dr Dorothy George pointed out in her *London Life in the Eighteenth Century* (1930), the parts of London in which the poor lived were also often the dangerous districts. In 1751 Henry Fielding observed that 'the late vast increase of the suburbs, the great irregularity of their buildings, the immense number of lanes, alleys, courts and bye-places, must think that had they been intended for the very purpose of concealment, they could not have been better contrived. Upon such a view the whole appears as a vast wood or forest in which the thief may harbour with as great security as wild beasts do in the deserts of Arabia or Africa.' Other factors contributed to the growth of the criminal districts: in particular the chaotic jurisdiction of the local authorities, and the lack of an adequate professional police force. But the criminal geography of London was certainly influenced by the expansion of confused networks of courts and alleys, the closely-packed and warren-like nature of the houses, and the tendency for their denizens to combine in order to thwart the prosecution of justice. In such districts the searching out and securing of offenders was a hazardous and sometimes hopeless procedure. In 1780 the houses in the Chick Lane, Field Lane and Black Boy Alley area, a notorious nest known familiarly as 'Jack Ketches Warren', were described as 'divided from top to bottom, and into many apartments, some having two, others three, others four doors, opening into different alleys. To such a height is our neglect of police arrived, the owners of these houses make no secret of their being let for the entertainment of thieves.'

Other dangerous areas could be found in Shoreditch, the Spittle, Southwark, the rookeries of St Giles, and the area between Golden Lane and Smithfield. The courts off Holborn and Gray's Inn Lane, off Great Queen Street and Long Acre, were also best avoided by the prudent, while a dangerous rookery, known first as 'the Bermudas', and subsequently as 'the Caribbee Islands', stretched between St Martin's Lane, Bedford Street and Chandos Street. Even many of the older parts of Westminster had an evil reputation. The courts leading off the Strand and the whole Covent Garden area were noted for their brothels and robberies, as well as for the theatres and gaming-houses. In 1766 Sir John Fielding ascribed the large number of brothels in Covent Garden partly to the presence of ruinous houses:

> One of the principal causes of the number of bawdy-houses being collected together in or near that parish, is there having been several estates in the courts and contiguous streets where the leases of the houses were so near expiring that it was not worth while to repair them till they were out, by which means they were let for almost nothing to the lowest of wretches, who hired three or four of them and filled them with common prostitutes. This made Exeter Street, Change Court, Eagle Court and Little Catherine Street so infamous that it was dangerous for persons to pass and repass.

Going east, Drury Lane and Russell Street were said to be infested with 'the most notorious characters' as the vacant houses in the theatre districts were readily converted into 'thieving shops for the reception of highwaymen, bullies, common assassins, and affidavit men'. A little further on, Clare Market and St Clement's Lane provided shelter for a host of beggars, and many disreputable courts opened off Fleet Market. Goodman's Fields was another theatre district with a reputation somewhat rivalling that of Covent Garden, and Houndsditch, parts of Whitechapel, Petticoat Lane and the riverside alleys stretching from St Katharine's to Limehouse were as unsafe as they were unsavoury.

Towards the end of the eighteenth century the character of crime in London underwent a change. By this time the more violent kinds of offences – armed robberies, assaults and murder – were declining. Footpads and highwaymen gave way to burglars as street lighting improved and the police became more efficient. Reform had begun in the middle of the century with the magistracy. The notorious 'trading justice' had used his court as a means of securing an income and, unfortunately, because the more honest sort of Middlesex magistrate left the

unending and disagreeable work of sitting regularly to the
trading justice, the courts became discredited as corrupt and
venal. As Dr George points out, Fielding's Justice Thrasher in
*Amelia* was not a caricature. However, the appointment of
Henry Fielding to Bow Street in 1749 marked a turning point.
'Fielding', says Dr George, 'made his office a public place for
the administration of justice instead of a justice-shop for
trafficking in fines and commitments, and set himself to
composing instead of inflaming "the quarrels of beggars and

114

'Bond and Judgement': a scene in a magistrate's court, 1779.

porters". He realized the terrible state of the poor and the perversities of the laws with the imaginative sympathy of a great novelist who was also a trained lawyer.'

Henry Fielding was succeeded by his brother John, who furthered the policy of attempting to save the young and reclaimable. It was he who persuaded the public to accept a professional police force which was openly dependent upon the central government. He also developed plans for sending young offenders to sea, and was closely connected with the foundation of the Marine Society in 1756. At length the attempts to get rid of the trading justice achieved success when the Act of 1792 restricted judicial business to seven public offices, each staffed by three paid magistrates and six paid constables. Six years later Patrick Colquhoun, another of the great London magistrates, and a friend of the philosopher and prison reformer, Jeremy Bentham, established the Thames Police Office. Thus London eventually acquired the basis for an effective system of stipendiary magistrates and police courts.

There was still, however, no central organization or direction, no sense of a comprehensive metropolitan police force designed to deal with London as a whole. Each London district had its own local magistrates, officials and constables, and their authority was essentially parochial. Part of the problem was the City of London which, with its own court, beadles and constables, was fundamentally opposed to any attempt to circumvent its ancient rights and administrative boundaries. Thus, although the police forces, both professional and amateur, at the disposal of the various authorities totalled some 3,000 men towards the end of the century, the system was effective only in dealing with local crimes, and even encountered difficulties in pursuing suspects from one side of the metropolis to the other. The force was inadequate for dealing with civil disorders of a major kind, such as the Gordon Riots. Then the troops had to be called in, with the resultant bloodshed. The forces of parochialism in London were strong and deep-rooted, and further advances in effective peace-keeping arrangements had to await Sir Robert Peel and his Metropolitan Police Act of 1829.

In the earlier part of the Georgian period the watchmen employed, even in the fashionable parts of London, were frequently so inept as to be characters of ridicule. Old, infirm men, badly paid, armed only with a long staff and a lantern – even their honesty was doubtful. 'Two of them', commented a resident, 'like honest fellows, handed me home to my chambers, without so much as stealing my hat or picking my

pockets, which was a wonder.' In the conditions of the time it took some courage to challenge a powerful robber or armed brawler. Many constables and night-watchmen, no doubt, took care to look the other way when something was afoot. Some watchmen, however, did their best to justify their pay. Court records show that there were active watchmen; and the magistrates, too, could show a determined spirit. J. T. Smith, in *Nollekens and His Times* (1829), tells how a magistrate made an arrest in person, and in a strikingly unusual manner:

> When the streets were entirely paved with pebblestones up to the houses, Hackneymen could drive their coaches close to the very doors. It happened that Mr Welch had good information, that a most notorious offender, who had for some time annoyed the Londoners in their walks through the green lanes to

The Watch to the rescue, as depict[ed] by Hogarth.

Mary-le-bone, and who had eluded the chase of several of his men, was in a first-floor of a house in Rose-street, Long-Acre. After hiring the tallest hackney-coach he could select, he mounted the box with the coachman, and when he was close against the house, he ascended the roof of the coach, threw up the sash of a first-floor window, entered the room, and actually dragged the fellow from his bed out at the window by his hair, naked as he was, upon the roof of the coach; and in that way carried the terror of the green lanes down New-street, and up St Martin's-lane, amidst the huzzas of an immense throng which followed him to Litchfield-street.

Some time before this, in the early 1730s, Jonathan Dickenson, a watchman in Cavendish Court, recounted to the judge how he and another watchman had taken a thief in nearby Little Marlborough Street:

As I called Two O'clock in Marlborough Street I found a Bar of some Pallisades bent, and looking farther I found another in the same Condition. Upon this I thought there was some Roguery going forward; so I planted my Lantern in the middle of Blenheim Street, that my Inhabitants might see I was upon my Duty, and then I went aside and stood upon the Watch and presently I heard a cry of stop Thief. Says I to my Brother Watch, do you go down Tyler Street and I'll go down Little Marlborough Street, and so we did. I met the Prisoner running with his drawn Sword (for he was a Soldier) and I knocked him down.

At this period the level of crime was such that, at the London Sessions held in the winter of 1732–33, a total of 87 prisoners were tried, of whom 6 hanged, 40 were transported, 2 were burned in the hand, 2 sentenced to small fines and imprisonment, and one, Bartholomew Harnet, was condemened for wilful and corrupt perjury 'to stand in the Pillory at the Royal Exchange, at the end of Chancery Lane in Fleet Street, and at the end of Old Bedlam in Bishopsgate Street, to suffer twelve months' imprisonment, and afterwards to be transported for seven years'. A case of armed robbery was tried at this Sessions, on 20 January 1733. The accusation was made by a Dr Stevens against three men, John Kemp, Samuel Elms and Ishmael Taylor. Dr Stevens laid his charge as follows, and his account well conveys the dangers of merely getting about in London 250 years ago:

I live in Covent Garden. On St Paul's Day in the Evening, I went with my Daughter to visit a Friend in Silver-Street. About Eleven I sent for a Hackney Coach, for as I expected to stay late I had discharged my own Chariot; the Coach waited at the Door about an hour and a half, and then I and my Daughter

The pillory at Charing Cross.

stept in. I suppose some Street Robbers had taken Notice of the
Coach's standing there so long; for at the End of Foster-lane
my Daughter told me there was a Couple of Men that follow'd
us. The Coach going faster in Cheapside, she observ'd that they
mended their Pace accordingly; Pappa! says she, how those
Gentlemen run! She took them to be Gentlemen, for they were
well dress'd. We went down Paternoster-Row, and in
Ave-Mary-Lane the Coach was stopp'd. A Man came to the
Coach-door, and holding a Pistol to my Daughter's Head, he
said, Don't be frightened Madam! but God damn you if you
squawl, I'll shoot you through the Head! I had a Purse with
10 Guineas in it, which I secur'd, and gave him only a half
Guinea, and a Spanish Dollar, which were loose in my Pocket.
God damn you, says he, you have more! No I ha'nt, says I,
you shall search me if you will. My Daughter gave him her
Purse; he ask'd her what was in it? She said, Not above 3 or 4
Guineas. And then he bid the Coachman drive on.

A similar robbery was described in court by a footman, Thomas
Watts. He stated:

I was behind the Coach when my Master was robbed; it was
about Eight O'clock on Monday night, betwixt Knightsbridge
and the Park-gate. I believe the Prisoner to be the Man; I
could distinguish his Person by the light of the Lanthorn; he
had a whitish great Coat on; he bid the Coachman stand, and
then went to the Window and bid them open it. Then he said,
Give me your Money; which I suppose was done, because I
heard him say, Is this all? Then he said, Give me your Sword.
My Mistress answered, My Father has none. And then he asked

for my Master's Watch and Ring, and I believe they were
delivered to him, but I do not know for certain. And about that
time I saw him make a Motion with his Hand in the Coach,
and he brought out my Master's Hat and Wig. A Man coming
along with a Lanthorn, I beckoned and spoke to him softly. He
came towards me, and I jumped down, and told him, that a
Highwayman was robbing my Master; the Light coming up, the
Prisoner turn'd his Horse and rode towards Knightsbridge.
That's the Man, says I; and so I and the other Man follow'd,
and alarm'd the People; but the Prisoner was not then taken . . .

A common sight in eighteenth-century London was the
public punishment of criminals. Minor offences resulted in an
hour or two exposed to public execration in the pillory, or a
whipping through the streets, bare-backed, at the tail of a cart.
Until 1783 hangings were in public, and the sight of felons in a
cart on their way to execution at Tyburn always drew throngs
of spectators who often treated 'Tyburn Fair' days as public
holidays, an occasion for jesting and making merry. A well-
known highwayman or a daring robber was often greeted with
cheers and applause at his last appearance, while a vicious
murderer faced groans, threats and insults from the bystanders.
There was little sense of the awful solemnity of the event. In
1739, for instance, the prosecutor of two men hung on Kennington Common for highway robbery 'rode at the tail of the
cart, jeering at them and insulting them all the way'. It was a
great free show, and one much relished by the eighteenth-
century crowd. The following, rather irreverent, anonymous
account is typical:

A condemned felon on his way to
Newgate philosophically disregards
the abuse of the mob.

The Press Yard at Newgate: a prisoner's fetters are struck off before he is
led away for execution (1821).

Mr Ordinary visits his melacholy flock at Newgate by eight. Doleful procession up Holborn Hill about eleven. Men handsome and proper, that were never thought so before, which is some comfort however. Arrive at the fatal place at twelve. Burnt brandy, women, and Sabbath-breaking repented of. Some few penitential drops fall under the gallows. Sheriffs men, parson, pickpockets, criminals, all very busy. The last concluding peremptory psalm struck up. Show over by one.

Descriptions of executions and the last speeches of the condemned were staple fare for the newspapers, and were hawked round the streets as broadsheets and ballads. Children even at a highly impressionable age might be taken to see a hanging. In *Nollekens and His Times* (1829), John Thomas Smith recalls when he was only 7 years old:

> Nollekens calling at my father's house in Great Portland-street, and taking me to Oxford-road to see the notorious Jack Rann, common called 'Sixteen-string Jack', go to Tyburn to be hanged for robbing Dr William Bell, in Gunnersbury-lane, of his watch and eighteen-pence in money; for which he received sentence of death on Tuesday the 26th of October 1774. The criminal was dressed in a pea-green coat, with an immense nosegay in the button-holes, which had been presented to him at St Sepulchre's steps; and his nankin small-clothes, we were told, were tied at each knee with sixteen strings. After he had passed, and Mr Nollekens was leading me home by the hand, I recollect his stooping down to me, and observing, in a low tone of voice, 'Tom, now, my little man, if my father-in-law, Mr Justice Welch, had been High-constable, we could have walked by the side of the cart all the way to Tyburn.'

Some of the condemned contrived to keep up a bold front, even on their last journey to Tyburn. One highwayman jokingly asked the sheriff's officer to order a diversion from the normal route so as to avoid passing a certain inn where, the highwayman said, he was sure to be recognized and arrested. The officer replied that in that event he would bail him. Others went to their deaths half-drunk, like the notorious Captain Kidd, and in a far from submissive mood. One highwayman refused to join the chaplain in prayers, and swore 'a great oath and kicked him and the hangman too off the cart'. It was not unusual for the condemned man to get himself carefully shaved and handsomely dressed for the occasion, in mourning or in the dress of a bridegroom. His friends provided a good coffin and flannel dress for his corpse, and he devoted some time to composing a last speech which he presented at the gallows, and which at his request was sometimes printed and circulated.

Swift has some trenchant lines about the last journey of 'Clever Tom Clinch':

> As clever Tom Clinch, *while the rabble was bawling,*
> *Rode stately through Holborn to die in his calling;*
> *He stopped at the* George *for a bottle of sack,*
> *And promised to pay for it when he'd come back.*
> *His waistcoat and stockings, and breeches were white,*
> *His cap had a new cherry ribbon to ty't;*
> *The maids to the doors and the balconies ran,*
> *And said, lack-a-day! he's a proper young man!*
> (*Poems,* 1747)

Generally five or six went together in the fatal cart, riding backwards with the rope round their necks. At the gibbet, after speeches, prayers and last farewells, the executioner fastened the rope to the crossbar, 'gives the horse a lash with

*Above* An execution outside Newgate, from a drawing by Rowlandson. The spectators seem prepared to enjoy themselves at this most gruesome of London's free shows.

An unusual occurrence at Tyburn: the condemned man is hurriedly cut down when a reprieve arrives five minutes after he had been 'turned off'.

his whip, away goes the cart, and there swings my gentleman kicking in the air'. If the hangman did not bother to pull on the victim's legs to put him out of his agony, this was done by friends and relations. 'They pull the dying person by the legs, and beat his breast to despatch him as soon as possible.' On one occasion, as related by James Guthrie, chaplain at Newgate, a condemned man actually managed to escape after the cart arrived at the gallows, though only to be recaptured and hastily executed. Guthrie's story is worth recounting at length:

> This John Davis dissembled and played the hypocrite egregiously, some days before his death . . . so that everybody thought him in a very dismal condition, as to his health; and he used to say that he did not think he should live to the time of his execution. The morning of his execution he was carried out on a man's back, and two or three men drag'd him into the cart like a dead lump, and out of compassion they did not tie his hands fast together, as is usually done. Under the tree he was tied up, but, as he pretended not able to stand (he hung upon and was supported by two or three men), he was loosed and suffered to sit down upon the cart in time of prayers, which hath been often done before in such cases . . . The prayers being over, they desired me to sing some verses of a psalm, and as I was beginning to sing at the 7th verse of the 16th psalm, he having a little before raised himself up, and sitting upon the cross tree of the cart, put his foot to the side of the cart, took hold of a spoke with his hand, and jumped over among the crowd in the twinkling of an eye. The officers and spectators were all of them surprised and astonished, and some of the people favouring his escape, he ran very fast till he got over a field. But the officers and some assistants pursuing hard, overtook him, and brought him back, two or three men holding and pushing him forward, with his coat off, his shirt and other clothes all torn, nothing on his head, and in this dismal condition they hurried him into the cart.

Even in the reign of George III (1760–1820), treason was still punishable by the medieval barbarism of hanging, drawing and quartering. After the '45, the last of the Jacobite risings, 38 rebel prisoners were publicly executed in this manner on Kennington Common. They hung for six minutes, were cut down while still alive, decapitated and disembowelled. Their heads decorated Temple Bar until they decomposed, and the last of these horrifying relics looked down on the passers-by in Fleet Street until 1772. As the century advanced support for a public display of the law's power declined, though many people, including Dr Johnson, thought a public execution had

The Pass Room at the Bridewell, a aquatint by Rowlandson and Pugin dated 1808. The beds consist of palle of straw piled up between partitions.

salutary effect, and regretted its passing. From 1783 Tyburn
·ll into disuse, and hangings were carried out in the yard of
Jewgate.

By this time, too, transportation was more frequently
·ubstituted for the death penalty, though it had its horrors as
·ell. Many of those transported never survived the voyage,
·nd only a handful ever came back after serving their sentence.
`ransportation, like the gallows, could mean a sentence of
·eath, as happened in the case of a Mr Eyre, a merchant 66
·ears of age, who was said to be worth the enormous sum of
·66,000. According to one contemporary account, Eyre

stole from pure covetousness, everything he could lay his hand
on. One day as he was endeavouring to hide under his cloak
two quires of paper, which he had seized, he was taken in the
fact and tried. So rich a thief, about to be condemned for the
value of a shilling, was really a phenomenon. The court was
crowded with people on the day of his trial. The theft was
proved, and the sentence of the judge condemned him to
transportation to America for seven years. This despicable being
was the just victim of his sordid avarice. His friends, in order to

lessen the inconvenience of the voyage, had . . .
procured him a cabin to separate him from the other convicts,
and bargained for his eating at the captain's table. Scarcely was
he at sea when he grudged the expense of this treatment, and
chose rather to lie on the straw with the other criminals than in
a good bed which he was obliged to pay for. Such sordid ideas
procured him no compassion from his fellow passengers; none
of them would have any intercourse with him, and he was
treated with general contempt. At last, the wretched being sunk
under the weight of years, of infirmities, and of the hardships he
had brought upon himself. He died before he reached America,
and his body was thrown into the sea.

The prisons of the period were notorious for their foul
conditions, their disease and squalor. Judges sat with herbs
strewn round their box as a precaution against the noxious
contagion of 'gaol fever'. Like the trading justices, the prison
wardens and turnkeys made a living from fees charged for
providing beds and better rooms, and for supplying food and
drink. Even when the keeper of Newgate clamped down on the
consumption of liquor in the prison, spirits were still smuggled
in by women 'who secrete them in such ways that it would be
termed the grossest insult to search for them'. The houses of
correction were sometimes used as recruiting centres for
emigrants to the colonies. The Clerkenwell House of Correction,
for example, was visited by the captain of a ship trading to
Jamaica, who plied the female inmates with drink in an
attempt to induce them to embark for the West Indies. Districts
around the prisons tended to spawn their own slums and
criminal habitats, linked directly or indirectly with the prisoners
incarcerated nearby. Before the building of Blackfriars Bridge
the area round Blackfriars was described in 1756 as filled with
'laystalls and bawdy houses, obscure pawnbrokers, gin-shops,
and alehouses; the haunts of strolling prostitutes, thieves and
beggars, who nestling thus in the heart of the City, become a
nuisance which it is worth all the money the bridge will cost
to remove'. One reason for the area's evil reputation was the
proximity of the 'terrible open sewer' of the River Fleet; and
even after the Fleet was covered over there remained the
shadow of the dismal walls of the Fleet, Ludgate and Newgate
prisons, as well as the Bridewell House of Correction.
Among the more gloomy sights of London for the curious
visitor were the debtors' prisons, such as the infamous Fleet
and Marshalsea prisons. It was estimated in 1716 that 60,000
debtors were imprisoned in England and Wales, a figure which
may not be wide of the mark. The Marshalsea Prison was

reported as accommodating more than 300 debtors in 1729, and many were in such straits that they literally starved to death. General Oglethorpe, the philanthropist and friend of Dr Johnson, raised subscriptions to pay off the debts of the more deserving and send them to South Carolina to make a fresh start. His committee reported that 'a day seldom passed without a death'. Vicious rogues who went by the name of 'tallymen' made a practice of trusting poor persons with goods, and when they failed to pay thrust them into prison 'with great charge for arrests and proceedings at law, which many times exceed the said debt'. Ruinous litigation was encouraged by rascally attorneys and bailiffs who profited from the fees. The families of debtors starved while waiting for a husband's or father's release; and the Fleet, said to be the largest brothel in the kingdom, had many children living in it. The Marshalsea was still in existence when Dickens was a boy, although by 1815 it had only 64 prisoners in it.

Ludgate was regarded as a more comfortable and rather more aristocratic sort of prison, inhabited by such unfortunate insolvents as beneficed clergy and attorneys at law. The fees paid by a prisoner on entering the prison amounted to 1s 2d; those due on leaving – assuming he was lucky enough to leave – 3s 2d, together with a shilling for the turnkey. For their maintenance the debtors paid 1s 2d a week if they were on the 'commons side' of the prison, or 1s 9d if on the superior 'Master's side'. Both at Ludgate and at the Fleet there were prisoners quite unable to pay maintenance for they were absolutely destitute. Such prisoners had to rely on charity. Prisoners took it in turn to solicit help by perambulating through the bounds of the prison and would rattle a box at a window grating overlooking Ludgate, crying: 'Pray remember the poor debtors!'

In the Georgian age, and for some time after, all institutions in which large numbers of people were herded together tended to be squalid, insanitary and unhealthy. Workhouses, designed under the Elizabethan Poor Law system as places where the able-bodied poor should be set to work in order to maintain themselves, had deteriorated by the eighteenth century into mere refuges, temporary shelters where the destitute were allowed to stay until they found help. They included many children, abandoned orphans, waifs and strays, who were supposed to be educated there until they were old enough to be apprenticed to a trade. It seems that the London Workhouse in Bishopsgate Street, established in 1698, was at least attempting early in the century to carry out its function of instilling in pauper children habits of regularity and industry. An admiring account of the workhouse's system of discipline tells of 30 or 40 children placed under a nurse in each ward, with two-tier bunks to sleep on, and each a 'flock bed, a pair of sheets, two blankets and a rug'. The day's routine was as follows:

> The bell rings at 6 o'clock in the morning to call up the children, and half an hour after the bell is rung for prayers, and breakfast; at 7 the children are set to work; 20 under a mistress to spin wool and flax, to knit stockings, to wind silk, to make and sew their linen, cloths, shoes, mark etc. All the children are called down for an hour every day to read, and an hour every day to write, 20 at a time.
>
> At 12 o'clock they go to dinner, and have a little time to play till one, then they are set to work again till 6 o'clock: They are rung to prayers, to their supper, and allowed to play till bedtime.

As time went on and the numbers of London's poor increased, the workhouses became even more overcrowded and decrepit. In the middle of the eighteenth century Clerkenwell Workhouse held more than twice the 150 inmates for whom it was built; the workhouse of St Martin's-in-the-Fields was said to be 'very ruinous and in danger of falling'; while the state of the St Paul's Shadwell Workhouse was so appalling that it 'should be taken down and rebuilt'. The nurses in charge of the children were generally old and dirty, and Jonas Hanway, the famous philanthropist, reported six or eight children crammed into a bed. In 1774 the parish workhouse of St Leonard's, Shoreditch, admitted having to put as many as 39 children into only three beds, 'by which means they contract disorders from each other'.

The poor law system was prodigal of children's lives. Few infants survived inside the workhouse, and those sent out to be cared for by parish nurses fared little better. A Parliamentary report of 1716 spoke of 'a great many poor infants and exposed bastard children ... inhumanly suffered to die by the barbarity of nurses, who are a set of people void of commiseration or religion, hired by the churchwardens to take off a burthen from the parish at the cheapest and easiest rates they can, and these know the manner of doing it effectually.'

Fortunately some hearts were touched by the plight of the infant paupers and by the sight of children lying exposed and dead in the street gutters. After 17 years of work on the problem, Thomas Coram, a sea-captain, obtained sufficient support to begin his Foundling Hospital. In 1742 the building

A view of the Foundling Hospital in Lamb's Conduit Fields in 1751, nine years after its foundation. Note the rural character of the surroundings.

in Lamb's Conduit Fields was begun. During the first 15 years of the Hospital's existence, 1,384 children were admitted, of whom only 724 died, an achievement which Hanway thought 'very remarkable' – a comment which sheds a ghastly light on the mortality rate in other institutions. After 1760 improvements in the Hospital resulted in a decline of the death rate among the foundlings, and by the end of the century it had fallen to less than one in six.

Meanwhile, Hanway was at work collecting statistics of the mortality of infants in the parish workhouses. The frightening figures – he found that of 275 children admitted in 1763 all but 19 had died within two years – enabled him to put pressure on Parliament to intervene. In 1767 a new measure compelled the parishes to send children out of London to be nursed; those under two were to be sent at least five miles from the cities of London and Westminster, and those under six at least three miles. Some enlightened parishes were already doing this: children from St James's, Westminster, were boarded out with carefully-selected cottagers on Wimbledon Common.

Those children who survived the rigours of infancy were eventually apprenticed to a trade. To take advantage of the

Law of Settlement parish officers did their best to apprentice the children in other parishes, for after 40 days had elapsed the child became the responsibility of the parish in which he was apprenticed. It was for this reason that numbers of London's pauper children were packed off to provide cheap labour for the early cotton mills in Derbyshire and the north. Since the premiums that had to be paid in order to apprentice children to prosperous, well-paid trades were usually high, it is not surprising that most paupers were apprenticed to badly-paid, sweated trades, the boys in tailoring, shoemaking, chimney-sweeping and other rough occupations, the girls in domestic service, various branches of dressmaking and needlework, or milk-selling in the streets. The Act obtained by Hanway in 1767 laid down that the premiums paid by the parish authorities should not be less than £4 2s, but this was a low figure which had frequently to be exceeded even in the poorer trades. Any person willing to provide maintenance and instruction could offer to take an apprentice, and too often the masters or mistresses were only interested in obtaining the premium and a supply of cheap labour. Many children became over-worked, underfed drudges in some unpleasant or blind-alley occupation.

In 1738 it was stated: 'The master may be a tiger in cruelty, he may beat, abuse, strip naked, starve and do what he will to the poor innocent lad, few people take much notice and the officer who put him out least of anybody.' The truth of this remark was demonstrated by the many cases of cruelty, rape, manslaughter and murder concerning apprentices which came before the courts. In one notorious case a Mrs Sarah Meteyard and her daughter were condemned and hung for the murder of a girl of 13, who had been consistently starved and beaten. Mrs Meteyard kept a haberdasher's shop in Bruton Street and took parish apprentices to work in a small close room making mittens and nets. Another infamous case of a similar nature in the 1760s concerned Mrs Brownrigg, a midwife living in Fetter Lane. She took in girl apprentices to serve as domestic drudges, but treated them so brutally that one ran away and another died. Some years earlier, John Bennett, a Thames fisherman from Hammersmith, was found guilty of the man-slaughter of his apprentice. The boy, aged 11, died of blows inflicted by a rope and a tiller, and suffered also from 'want of looking after and hunger and cold together'. Neglect, ill-treatment and hardship were the common lot of parish apprentices. The unhealthy, corrupting and dangerous conditions in which they were employed, especially in tailoring, street-selling, domestic service, shops and chimney-sweeping, were not fully remedied until well into the Victorian era, and even into the present century. One of the last measures to deal specifically with parish apprentices, Peel's Health and Morals of Apprentices Act of 1802, was concerned with conditions in the relatively new field of textile factories. Although not very effective, it proved to be the first of a long series of acts regulating factory employment in the nineteenth century.

The scandal of expectant mothers and young babies in workhouses led to the provision of lying-in hospitals. The first of these appeared in 1749, and very considerable success was achieved in reducing the appallingly high mortality rates all too common at this time. The eighteenth century, in fact, saw a very remarkable growth in the number of hospitals. Such ancient foundations as St Bartholomew's in Smithfield and St Thomas's in Southwark, were extended in size and improved in facilities. New hospitals appeared: the Westminster in 1720, and Guy's, endowed by the wealthy Lombard Street bookseller,

'The Asylum for the Deaf', a water-colour by John Collet.

Thomas Guy, five years later. In 1734 the building of S
George's Hospital was begun on its commanding site at Hyde
Park Corner, then a rustic spot on London's outskirts. The
London Hospital in the East End was opened in 1740, moved
to the Whitechapel Road in 1752, and subsequently was much
extended. The Middlesex, first established in Windmill Street
near Tottenham Court Road in 1745, was later removed to its
present site, and by the early years of the nineteenth century
provided ten times its original number of 18 beds.

However, conditions in Georgian hospitals left a great deal
to be desired. Patients suffering from all sorts of complaints,
some of them infectious, were blithely mixed up together in
general wards. Nurses had little training or skill, and were
often 'of a low sort', not being above getting into bed with,
presumably, the healthier of the male patients. Hygiene and
sanitation were grossly neglected, and the wooden beds were
dirty and infested with vermin. 'Hospital fever', akin to 'workhouse fever' and 'gaol fever', in other words typhus, periodi-
cally ravaged the wards. Some hospitals demanded from
incoming patients a deposit or security to cover possible burial
charges, a precaution which not only discouraged those
admitted but also effectively excluded the poorer class of
people. Despite all the defects there is some evidence, however,
of improving standards, and it seems that a remarkably high
proportion of patients were discharged restored to health.
The hospitals were important, too, as schools of medicine and
surgery, and as centres of clinical practice.

Those excluded from hospitals by poverty could still get
useful help at dispensaries, institutions which served as centres
for advice and free medicine. The first dispensary was opened
in Red Lion Square in 1769 'for the relief of the infant poor' –
it helped to popularize improved 'bubby-pots' or feeding
bottles; in 1770 came the General Dispensary, and subsequently many others followed, both in London and in the
provinces. They were said to be effective in teaching element-
ary hygiene, encouraging people, for example, to practise
greater cleanliness and to admit fresh air into sick rooms. They
were also centres for innoculation and, from 1798, of vaccination against smallpox. Dispensaries also began to develop
measures to deal with the common plague of typhus. It was
recognized that fever cases should be carefully isolated, and
this led eventually to the first isolation hospital, the London
House of Recovery, opened in Gray's Inn Road in 1802.
Houses infected by fever were whitewashed with hot lime and
fever cases were admitted to the hospital immediately, without

he customary delay while a subscriber's letter was furnished.
teps were taken to clean up well-known fever spots, and
hether because of these or other factors, after the turn of the
entury the incidence of deaths from typhus declined. By the
nd of the eighteenth century even some workhouse infirmaries
ere adopting enlightened methods of treating sickness. At
Iarylebone, in particular, Dr Rowley was advocating bathing,
esh air and scrupulous cleanliness.

The plight of poor lunatics remained desperate well into the
ictorian period. Well-to-do families could place their de-
anged relations in private institutions, though it was argued
aat this might sometimes be done – and it could easily be
rranged – for sinister reasons. The pauper lunatic was con-
ned to a dirty cell, or kept, perhaps chained to the wall, in a
oom with other paupers. The old hospital provided specially
r lunatics was Bethlehem, commonly known as Bedlam,
hich had been built on the south side of Moorfields in 1676.

Bedlam, from Hogath's *A Rake's Progress*, 1735.

131

Over the gate were two figures, 'curiously carved', representing respectively raving and melancholy madness. Early in the eighteenth century it was said that 'the diet is very good and wholesome, being commonly boiled beef, mutton or veal, and broth with bread for dinners on Sundays, Tuesdays, and Thursdays, the other days bread, cheese and butter, or on Saturdays, peas pottage, rice milk, fermity, or other pottage; and for suppers they usually have broth or milk pottage, always with bread; and there is this farther care taken, that some of the committee go weekly to the said hospital to see the provisions weighed, and that the same be good and rightly expended.' The hospital came to be regarded as one of the curiosities of London. Eighteenth-century visitors made it a regular part of their itinerary. After the Tower and the tombs in Westminster Abbey, they went on to see 'the poor mad folk in Bedlam'.

*Above* The cockpit, as depicted Hogarth, 1759.

A public that was so insensitive as to consider the wild ravings and distorted grimaces of the lunatics in Bethlehem a sight worthy for tourists was equally indifferent to the savagery of many popular amusements. These included bull-baiting, bear-baiting, dog-fighting, throwing at cocks and cock-fighting, wrestling and cudgel play. There was also boxing, in which the bouts lasted scores of rounds until the pugilists battered one another into insensibility. Some female prize-fighters took the ring, and the exploits of the more celebrated, such as the fearsome Bruising Peg, were keenly followed by the sporting crowds. Early in the century there were three bear-gardens, at Hockley-in-the-Hole, Clerkenwell, in Marylebone Fields at the back of Soho Square, and at Tothill Fields, Westminster. Cockpits were attached to many a disreputable inn, but the most famous were on the south side of St James's Park and near Gray's Inn Gardens. The typical cockpit consisted of tiers of benches surrounding a raised platform where the cocks, matched by weight and specially prepared for the fray, were set to tear each other to pieces. Sometimes the cocks fought with silver spurs, but more generally with the common steel ones. All these sports were supported by the common people as well as by gentlemen fond of a wager, and large sums changed hands at the Royal Cockpit in St James's Park, and at the less fashionable venues.

In the late eighteenth century public taste and morals gradually changed. There was still enormous indifference to suffering and brutality, but the taste for the more savage sports, like the more savage forms of punishment, gradually waned. In the early decades of the new century a number of bills were

unsuccessfully put before Parliament to abolish certain blood sports, and the efforts of the reformers eventually bore fruit in the form of the Cruelty to Animals Act of 1835. Opposition to sports like bull-baiting, patronized mainly by the working classes, arose partly from a more puritanical attitude towards work and leisure. Sir William Pulteney maintained that the sport was 'cruel and inhuman; it drew together idle and disorderly persons; it drew also from their occupations many who ought to be earning subsistence for themselves and families; it created many disorderly and mischievous proceedings, and furnished examples of profligacy and cruelty.'

Cockfighting was still much in vogue, however, when James Boswell came to town in the early years of the reign of George III. On 15 December 1762 Boswell decided to go and see a cockfight, though it is clear from his diary that he considered it a somewhat disreputable thing to do:

> At five I filled my pockets with gingerbread and apples (quite the method), put on my old clothes and laced hat, laid by my watch, purse, and pocket-book, and with oaken stick in my hand sallied to the pit. I was too soon there. So I went into a low inn, sat down amongst a parcel of arrant blackguards, and drank some beer . . .
>
> I then went to the Cockpit, which is a circular room in the middle of which the cocks fight. It is seated round with rows gradually rising. The pit and the seats are all covered with mat. The cocks, nicely cut and dressed and armed with silver heels, are set down and fight with amazing bitterness and resolution. Some of them were quickly dispatched. One pair fought three quarters of an hour. The uproar and noise of betting is prodigious. A great deal of money made a very quick circulation from hand to hand. There was a number of professed gamblers there. An old cunning dog whose face I had seen at Newmarket sat by me a while. I told him I knew nothing of the matter. 'Sir,' said he, 'you have as good a chance as anybody.' He thought I would be a good subject for him. I was young-like. But he found himself balked. I was shocked to see the distraction and anxiety of the betters. I was sorry for the poor cocks. I looked round to see if any of the spectators pitied them when mangled and torn in a most cruel manner, but I could not observe the smallest relenting sign in any countenance.

The coarser kind of amusements were connected with the proliferation of low inns and grog-shops, where cheap spirits were retailed. The sickening squalor of the gin age is vividly portrayed in Hogarth's 'Gin Lane', and in reality it was certainly horrifying. The 'gin orgy' was at its height between 1720 and the middle of the century, though the consumption of

Hogarth's famous 'Gin Lane'. Above the arch in the bottom left-hand corner a notice reads: 'Drunk for a Penny, Dead drunk for two Pence, Clean Straw for Nothing'.

cheap spirits had been increasing since the end of the seventeenth century. The orgy was fed by the sheer cheapness of the spirits and the ease of obtaining them. 'Brandy and Geneva shops', where people could tipple and get drunk for a copper or two, multiplied. They were held to be responsible for many crimes of violence, neglected children, incapable workmen and the spread of infectious diseases. Sales of gin soared from $3\frac{1}{2}$ million gallons in 1727 to nearly $6\frac{1}{2}$ million gallons in 1735. By 1743 over twice as much was being drunk as 15 years before. In the metropolitan area of Middlesex alone there were said to be over 7,000 retailers of gin and brandy. It was impossible to obtain an accurate figure because the constables making the returns were themselves often gin-sellers. Already in 1726 gin was being sold by 'chandlers, many tobacconists, and such who sell fruit or herbs in stalls or wheelbarrows', as well as by 'many more who sell privately in garrets, cellars, back rooms and other places . . .'

In an attempt to reduce the evil an Act passed in 1736 imposed a heavy duty of £1 a gallon on spirits, and required retailers to take out an annual licence costing as much as £50. It was expected that as a result of this Act the revenue from duties would fall by some £70,000 a year, and heavy rioting was envisaged. But as it turned out the Act could not be enforced – the mob hunted down and murdered those who informed on illicit retailers. In 1743 a more realistic measure reduced the cost of the licence to £1, but restricted it to those who already had an alehouse licence. Consumption fell temporarily, but went up again when distillers were exempted from the Act and allowed to sell retail, a concession which opened the way to much illicit liquor selling. A really effective control came only in 1751, when increased duty made spirits less cheap, and distillers, grocers and chandlers were forbidden to retail. Chandlers had been especially important in spreading the gin habit, for they stocked the common household necessities – candles, soap, coal, cheese – which brought the housewife and maid-servant into their shops daily. With higher duties, and occasional prohibitions on distilling when grain was scarce, gin consumption fell to a more restrained level, though it was still heavy. The Act of 1751 also prohibited the sale of gin in prisons, but this evil, too, could not be stamped out. In 1776 as much as 120 gallons of gin were sold weekly in the King's Bench Prison, in addition to other spirits, and eight butts (barrels) of beer. The Fleet Prison saw many nights of 'riots and drunkenness', and the debtors in Newgate sent out invitations to both inmates and outsiders to join in gatherings

their rooms where drink would be sold.

Gin drinking, says Dr George, in her book *London Life in the eighteenth Century*, 'was essentially a disease of poverty. Gin was so cheap, so warming and brought such forgetfulness of cold and misery.' It was the drink, particularly, of the more sedentary trades, weavers, for instance, and of women. It was rife among the beggars and inmates of workhouses and prisons. Labouring men and artisans doing heavy work preferred beer, and as gin rose in price with increased duties there was a swing towards greater consumption of beer. Colquhoun's figures for licensed houses at the end of the eighteenth century – 825 in the City, 957 in Westminster and 759 in Holborn – show a marked decline on the estimated numbers for the mid-century. Drunkenness persisted as a characteristic of the poorer areas of London, and gin remained the weakness of many a housewife, but the worst excesses of 50 years earlier had gone for good.

To that extent, and with the gradual decline of brutal sports, the London of George IV had become a more sober, less savage city. Crime was still endemic and still inadequately checked, and there was still great suffering among the neglected children and sick of the poor. But there were already significant signs of progress, and London was moving unmistakably into the age of reform.

'The Gin Shop', by George Cruikshank, 1829. Although the gin orgy had by this time long passed away, cheap spirits continued to be the ruin of many of the poor.

135

# 6 The Workers' London

'Our supreme governors, the mob.'
Horace Walpole, in a letter to Horace Mann, 7 September 1743

The Georgian age in London was the age of the mob. Cheap drink, inadequate police, widespread crime and brutalizing sports all contributed to the frequency with which violence erupted on the streets. Any foreigners of outlandish appearance were prone to attract the attention of idle loungers, and Jew-baiting was at one time a popular sport in the poorer areas. After a murder in Chelsea, for which four Jews were hung, any Jew, as Francis Place recalled, was liable to be 'hooted, hunted, cuffed, pulled by the beard, spit upon, and so barbarously assaulted in the streets, without any protection from the passers-by or the police, as seems when compared with present times, almost impossible to have existed at any time'. According to Place, the appearance in London in 1787 of a celebrated Jewish boxer, Daniel Mendoza, brought about a change for the better. Jewish pugilists, such as Mendoza, Dutch Sam and Young Dutch Sam, became popular heroes, and the new scientific school of boxing introduced by Mendoza meant that it was no longer quite as safe to interfere with Jews, at least with the younger ones.

Hostility towards foreigners in general seems to have declined in the second half of the century. The more ancient and more common cause of mob violence was high bread prices. From the 1750s dearer bread became the norm as the country's growing population put increased pressure on grain supplies. The demand for food tended to grow faster than the supply, despite the enclosure of open fields and wastes, and despite, too, the introduction by farmers of improved methods of cultivation and better breeds of livestock. As a result food prices rose and indeed towards the end of the century reached unprecedented levels.

The problem was exacerbated by the greater frequency of bad harvests. In the first half of the century bad harvests were rare, though the disastrously cold winter and spring of 1739–40 sent prices suddenly soaring. Towards the end of the century bad harvests and high prices were more frequent, and during the long Revolutionary and Napoleonic Wars (1793–1815) the extraordinary runs of very bad seasons resulted in prices reaching famine levels. The significance of the harvest becomes obvious when it is remembered that the working man's family spent some three-fifths or more of their income on food, of which bread was by far the chief item, especially among the very poor. Indeed, some low-paid workers may have spent as much as half their income on bread alone. For them, for the old and infirm, the street-sellers and beggars, a rise in the price of bread was a disaster.

*Above* Gillray's portrayal of Daniel Mendoza, the noted Jewish pugilist.

*Opposite* The effects of war on trade, rises in the cost of food and drink, the threat to livelihood posed by new products or machinery, or merely an increase in the price of theatre seats might all serve to spark off a riot in eighteenth-century London. Notorious swindlers also attracted hostility: here angry sailors robbed of their watches and money in Peter Wood's brothel, the Star Tavern off the Strand, are bent on revengeful destruction of his premises (1749).

In the expensive times, such as the end of the eighteenth century, it is not surprising that the mob rampaged against corn merchants, millers and flour wholesalers, and attacked the wealthy in their coaches. At these times there was much resentment against the open flaunting of wealth, and it was dangerous for well-dressed persons to walk about in some parts of London. In 1800, when bread was very scarce and dear, John Rusby, a jobber of the Corn Exchange in Mark Lane, was convicted of 'regrating' (re-selling grain in the same market on the same day). The case attracted much publicity, and the mob, far from being placated by the conviction, was inflamed to riot. Rusby's house was pulled down, and Rusby himself was fortunate to escape with his life. Several weeks later a mob proceeded to Mark Lane and demanded the lowering of grain prices. Fortunately 'the ready attendance of the volunteers, and the firmness of their countenance, alarmed the populace, and, without the actual use of firearms, repressed the commotions'.

Before the end of the eighteenth century, however, dear food was no longer the prime cause of rioting, though it may have contributed in some years to the unrest arising from other economic factors and political conditions. London workers were particularly sensitive to any threat to their established standards of wages and employment. A usual cause of trouble was the appearance of rival products imported from abroad, or made in a new way at home, so taking work away from existing craftsmen. Thus, in 1719 and 1720, the Spitalfields silk-weavers, renowned for their bellicosity, ignored the restraining hand of the Weavers' Company and took to the streets against cheap imported 'calimancoes'. The 'calico madams', bold ladies who dared to sport the new cloth in weavers' districts, were liable to have the clothes torn off their backs or have acid thrown at them. Some particularly serious incidents resulted in the Act of 1720 which prohibited all use of the offending material and, for the time being at least, restored tranquillity to the weaving-sheds and workshops of Spitalfields and Whitechapel. Sixteen years later, in the summer of 1736, there were again serious riots in the East End of London, when the weavers and other workers protested against the use of cheap Irish labour. Anti-Irish sentiment was so violent that the troops had to be called out. These riots, though primarily concerned with cut-price labour, had a background of suspicion about Jacobite influence, two factors easily connected in many people's minds with the Catholic Irish immigrants.

138

In the middle of the eighteenth century sporadic unrest over wages, cheap labour, rival products, new machinery, working conditions and similar matters were commonplace. Any change in prices might spark off trouble, as when increased duties raised the price of gin. Even a rise in the price of theatre seats brought on riots, and during the wars with France there were noisy scenes when French artistes appeared on stage. Covent Garden and Drury Lane installed barriers of iron spikes along the front of the stage to provide the actors with some protection from rowdy patrons.

In the 1760s, and particularly in the later years of the decade, industrial unrest rose to new heights, a development possibly connected with the prevalent higher food prices. Workmen formed combinations and went on strike, demonstrated in processions, sent employers threatening letters phrased in bloodcurdling terms, destroyed unpopular machinery, and made attacks on hostile individuals and their property. Sailors, discharged in their thousands at the end of the Seven Years' War in 1763, petitioned Parliament and, with greater effect, prevented ships from sailing and forced employers to raise seamen's wages. Others who protested in the mid 1760s included watermen, coopers, hatters, glass-grinders, sawyers, tailors, coal-heavers and silk-weavers. The London journeymen tailors had been trying to establish a permanent union since the 1720s, and in support of their long-standing efforts to secure better wages and conditions 2,000 of them marched to Parliament in 1768 with a petition. In this disturbance-ridden year the coal-heavers of Shoreditch and Wapping stopped unloading the lighters in support of higher pay. There were riots resulting in deaths and injuries. Publicans who acted as the coal-heavers' agents were attacked, and sailors brought in to unload the colliers were assaulted. Several of the coal-heavers were arrested and sentenced for their part in the affrays, and seven were hanged in Stepney, while 300 soldiers struggled to control a crowd said to number 50,000.

In the same destructive year, 1768, the weavers were once more out in the streets. In disguise, at dead of night, and armed with pistols and cutlasses, they broke into the houses of those workmen who operated the hated engine-looms, destroying both machines and silks. The masters also came in for their share of violence when they attempted to reduce the weavers' piece-rates. Attacks on masters and machines continued in the following year, until the government went to the length of quartering troops in Spitalfields, and two of the weavers' leaders were caught and hanged at Bethnal Green. Unrest still continued, but to a lesser degree, and in 1773 the Spitalfields Act gave magistrates the power to fix wage rates in the silk-weaving trade and to see that they were enforced. Sailors were on the rampage again at the close of the American War in 1783, but in general the period between the early 1770s and the outbreak of the Revolutionary Wars in 1793 was one of relative industrial peace.

As Professor Rudé remarks, the Englishman's right to his daily bread and to his 'birthright' of 'liberty' 'were the main motors (and at times the twin motors) of popular disturbance in Hanoverian London'. It followed that almost any event in the economic or political spheres might cause rioting. Indeed many of the popular causes were political, such as hostility to Walpole's excise scheme, to the regulation of gin, the War of Jenkins's Ear, and to relaxations of the penal laws concerning Roman Catholics. The serious industrial unrest of the 1760s coincided with the agitation surrounding John Wilkes and the question of the liberty of the press. The Wilkite agitation, although it also came to a head in 1768 and 1769, the years of London's worst industrial unrest, was really a separate issue from the bread-and-butter questions which inflamed the industrial workers at that time. The Wilkes case contributed, no doubt, to the atmosphere of disturbance and challenge to authority, and the threats to liberty which his case provoked could be seen as related in some sense to the current concern about wages and employment. But on the whole the two sets of issues were coincidental rather than systematically connected.

Wilkes, a Member of Parliament, achieved notoriety in 1763 when he published in issue No 45 of his journal, the *North Briton*, an attack on the King's speech, an attack which the government claimed to be a seditious libel. Wilkes was arrested on a general warrant, then a fairly common practice, though he was shortly released and subsequently proceeded to obtain damages for unlawful arrest. However, he was unwise enough to reprint his famous issue No 45, as well as an obscene parody of Pope's *Essay on Man*. The Commons summoned him to explain himself but Wilkes fled abroad, and did not reappear in London until the general election of March 1768. His return was a signal for popular outbursts, his enthusiastic followers chairing him through the streets with strident cries of 'Wilkes and Liberty'.

Wilkes next managed to be re-elected to Parliament as the Member for the county of Middlesex. Again there was enthusiasm, now on an even greater scale. His ebullient supporters ran through the streets forcing householders to light their windows

Hogarth's portrait of John Wilkes 'drawn from the life and etch'd in aquafortis', 1763.

celebration of his victory, on pain of having their glass broken. Among those who were too slow or too obstinate to respond were Lord Bute and several other noblemen, as well as a number of City gentlemen. The windows of the Mansion House were shattered, and every door from Temple Bar to Hyde Park Corner had 'No 45' scrawled on it in chalk. Wilkes now surrendered to the authorities, and on a variety of minor offences was sent to prison for 22 months. On his way to the King's Bench a crowd surrounded his coach, took out the horse and dragged the vehicle through Temple Bar into the City. To loud cheering Wilkes appeared at an upper window of the Three Tuns Tavern in Spitalfields, before leaving in disguise and under cover of darkness, to give himself up to his gaolers. Crowds of his followers gathered round the prison, where there were further disturbances. On the day of the opening of Parliament the crowd came to see if he would be allowed to leave the prison and take his seat. Stones were thrown at the troops, who opened fire, killing and wounding a score of people. This 'massacre' as it was called, was followed by renewed rioting, the houses of magistrates were damaged, and again the windows of the Mansion House suffered. In March the following year the radical mob attacked a procession of merchants who were going to deliver a loyal address to the King. Only a few of the coaches managed to run the gauntlet of St James's Palace, and those which succeeded were 'so daubed with dirt, and shattered, that both masters and drivers were in the utmost peril of their lives'.

During his imprisonment Wilkes increased his popular support by turning out a stream of letters and proclamations. In his absence he was elected a city alderman, and an influential group of City figures gathered round him. In 1769 he was again expelled from Parliament, was re-elected by his Middlesex supporters, and yet again his election was declared null and void. On his third election by the Middlesex voters his opponent – beaten despite Wilkes's absence by more than 800 votes – was declared by an exasperated Parliament to have been duly elected.

Wilkes, by now released from prison, was probably the moving spirit behind the famous 'printers' case' which next inflamed popular opinion. A number of London newspapers were printing reports of speeches and proceedings in Parliament despite a rule to the contrary, and the Commons proceeded to prosecute the printers concerned. Again Wilkes triumphed. In due course he rose through the offices of Sheriff and Alderman to become, in 1774, London's Lord Mayor, an event which provoked the last popular outburst of his career.

Wilkes was in some respects primarily self-seeking and ambitious, and with his Lord Mayor's eminence he had reached his objective. For a number of years his unhandsome face enlivened proceedings in the Commons, and he continued to propound his radical doctrines. His days as a popular leader were over, however. His career, for all its use of the mob and disregard of the law, produced three important advances in enlarging the liberties of Englishmen. Arrest by general warrant was ended and declared illegal; the right of electors to return the candidate of their choice was endorsed; and the open reporting of Parliamentary debates became an established function of the press. The radical movement of which Wilkes was part was now beginning to put the forces of Parliamentary reform in motion, and in these years the first small steps were being taken towards the Reform Act of 1832. Wilkes's career up to his election as Lord Mayor served as a focus for radical views among the middle ranks of townsmen. He could attract the enthusiasm of the ordinary journeymen and the poor, and knew how to make the most of it; but for all his popularity with the mob, Wilkes's main core of support was among the London merchants and shop-keepers – not the wealthy bankers and financiers, but the lesser sort of commercial men, industrialists, and craftsmen. It was these people who continued in later years to provide the principal body of support for the radicalism of the Revolutionary Wars and their disturbed aftermath.

But, more immediately, the political turbulence that surrounded the career of the flamboyant Wilkes took in 1780 a far more sinister and destructive turn. Two years earlier Parliament had passed the Catholic Relief Act, a measure designed to remove certain of the restrictions and penalties under which Catholics had laboured since the end of the previous century. In London, a little-known and unbalanced nobleman, Lord George Gordon, headed a newly-formed Protestant Association, which had as its object the repeal of the new Act, a purpose which found popularity with many Londoners, and one which had already been espoused by the Common Council of the City. When anti-Catholic feeling burst out into rioting a dangerous situation arose because some magistrates and constables had already signed the Protestant Association's petition, and were reluctant to take firm measures to restrain the mob. Only when it became obvious that the rioting was getting out of hand, and that the Bank of England and the Mansion House were ambitious

The Gordon Riots: the mob burning Newgate Prison, 7 June 1780.

...argets in the mob's course of destruction, were the City authorities forced into stronger measures to protect life and property.

The terrible Gordon Riots, the most bloody outbursts of this turbulent age, erupted on 2 June 1780. The respectable, if bigoted, Protestant tradesmen who formed the main body of support were soon joined by a mass of lower wage-earners, many of whom, like the Spitalfields weavers, had a long tradition of street rioting. The trouble began in Westminster when the crowd greeted Members of Parliament with shouts of 'No Popery!' Soon bands of rioters broke off to attack and burn the property of well-known Catholics, and on subsequent days there were further gatherings and outrages. Catholic houses and chapels were pillaged, and Justice Hyde, who read the Riot Act, had his house destroyed in return. The mob next turned their attention to Newgate. They broke down the gates and cell-doors, released the prisoners, and set the place on fire. The next to suffer was the Sessions House at the Old Bailey. Lord Mansfield, who had sentenced Wilkes 12 years before, and was known to be a keen supporter of the Catholic Relief Act, had his house plundered and his precious library destroyed. On the worst day, Wednesday 7 June, the rioters went to new lengths, attacking the premises of Catholic merchants, shop-keepers and justices. That evening they broke into the distilleries of Thomas Langdale, where over 100,000 gallons of gin were stored. The vats caught fire, and helped by the flood of gin the flames soon spread to neighbouring houses.

This did not mark the end of the riots. The mob released the prisoners from the Fleet Prison, and the King's Bench and other prisons on the south side of the river were set on fire. The tollhouses at Blackfriars Bridge were attacked for their half-pence, and an attempt to storm the Bank of England was repulsed by the troops stationed at the Royal Exchange. Further attacks on Catholic shops, inns and houses continued next day, but the violence was at last dissipating. The troops were now in the streets in force, and old John Wilkes, who knew a thing or two about riots, was prominent in the force called up by the London Military Association. Some 450 people were arrested, and Lord George Gordon was shut up in the Tower. In the end, 160 were brought to trial and 25 of them hanged. Far more, over 200, were killed in the streets by the troops, another 75 died in hospital and 173 were wounded. Fifty buildings were destroyed or badly damaged, and £100,000 was paid out in compensation.

The Gordon Riots, as Professor Rudé points out, were not just the effects of blind mass-hysteria. As with other great political disturbances of the period, the bands of rioters had a degree of organization. They collected round a nucleus of local men, and followed the orders given by a temporary leader or captain. Attacks on property were directed at carefully selected victims. Even in the Gordon Riots care was taken to avoid damaging other property, and the lives that were lost all came from the ranks of the rioters; none occurred among the rioters' targets. The bulk of the rioters, too, were by no means the riff-raff of the slums. Of those who came to trial, two out of three were wage-earners, journeymen, apprentices, small masters, domestic servants and labourers – men who rarely had a criminal record but were settled, apparently sober, citizens. The most riotous areas, similarly, were not those of the worst slums or criminal haunts but respectable districts in the City, the Strand, Southwark, Shoreditch and Spitalfields. The victims were not the poor Catholic workers of the East End, but the more well-to-do Catholic merchants and publicans.

Radical activity and political unrest did not end with Wilkes and the Gordon Riots. The sympathy of reformers for the objectives of the revolutionaries in France influenced the corresponding societies, organizations formed to discuss reform of the constitution, which flourished in London and many provincial towns in the 1790s. The Corresponding

Society of London had as its secretary John Frost, an attorney, but the bulk of the members were artisans and shopkeepers, men like John Lovett, a hairdresser, Richard Hodgson, a master hatter, and John Bone, a Holborn bookseller. When England moved from cautious approval of the French Revolution to hostility against its excesses, and then to open war, the corresponding societies came under suspicion. In 1793 Frost was sent to prison for expressing support for the French, and Margarot, the London Society's president, was sentenced to transportation for his part in planning assistance for the French in case of a possible invasion. However, the acquittal on a charge of high treason of Hardy, a founder of the London Society, Horne Tooke, Thelwall, and other leading figures, sparked off mass expressions of enthusiasm for the radical cause, events not a little influenced by the bad harvest and high food prices of 1795. The government passed the Seditious Meetings Act, and for a time the London Society adopted a more restrained role. In 1798 there were further outbreaks of severe unrest, and the Combination Acts were passed to suppress the corresponding societies, workers' trade unions and similar organizations. The radicals, however, achieved a remarkable victory in 1807 when Burdett and Cochrane won the Westminster election of that year. The Westminster Committee of radical politicians remained as a model for similar organizations elsewhere, and many of the names associated with it – Burdett, Cartwright, Cobbett, Hunt and Place – were to be, in the words of Edward Thompson, 'prominent in the history of articulate Radicalism in the next fifteen years'.

With peace came unemployment and renewed distress, and in the early post-war years there was widespread unrest. The country was full of rumours of seditious meetings, plans for armed insurrections and the existence of numerous government spies. Some believed revolution was imminent. Wordsworth warned the Prime Minister that if the troops were withdrawn from the capital 'four and twenty hours would not elapse before the tri-coloured flag would be placed upon Carlton House'. Alarm was spread by reports of the Luddite machine-breakers of the midlands, and the more limited protests of rural bread-rioters in the eastern counties. The Blanketeers, a group of Lancashire weavers some 600 strong, set out from Manchester to petition the Prince Regent on the depressed state of the cotton trade.

Late in 1816, a few months before the Blanketeers began their abortive march, the famous Spa Fields gatherings occurred in the capital. These mass assemblies came together to hear well-known speakers, such as 'Orator' Hunt, argue the case for reform. The crowds were probably influenced by the current unrest – London was full of discharged soldiers and sailors – and the more extreme radicals saw in the great numbers attracted an opportunity of furthering wider aims. At the second meeting, on 2 December 1816, a contingent of the huge crowd addressed by Hunt made for the Tower, where they unavailingly called upon the troops to join them. Other groups broke away to loot the gunsmiths' shops. Rather than sparking a revolution, however, the Spa Fields riots effectively threw the reform movement into disarray. The threatening activities of some small sections of the vast crowds gave the government good grounds for taking sterner measures against the reformers.

There followed a confused period of renewed alarms, widespread reports of arming and drilling, and intense activity among the various leaders and factions of the radical movement. The government decided on stronger measures. In 1819, as Sidmouth's Six Acts designed to regulate public meetings and stamp out seditious literature were going through Parliament, a group of extremists prepared a new move which they hoped would bring about a general uprising. These were the Cato Street conspirators, led by Arthur Thistlewood, a seasoned radical activist and republican. The plot was to assassinate the entire cabinet as an act of revenge for the notorious 'Peterloo Massacre' in Manchester the previous August. It failed miserably. The plan was known to the government long before, and in February 1820 the authorities pounced. Thistlewood and his fellow-conspirators were arrested, tried and executed. The main consequence of this sensation was to justify the government's policy of repression, and perhaps to show the futility of radical extremism. But the more moderate reformers, such as Cobbett and Hunt, were unabashed, and continued to write and preach reform. As the post-war depression lifted and economic conditions improved, the more violent forms of protest died down. Radical agitation, however, continued, and for the last years of George III's reign and during the short reign of George IV (1820–30) the political scene remained turbulent.

It was the normally respectable workmen who had run amok through London in the Gordon Riots of 1780. Below them existed a mass of itinerant street hawkers, beggars, vagrants, petty criminals, pickpockets and prostitutes. This underworld was occasionally glimpsed in affrays concerned

*Top* The arrest of the Cato Stre conspirators on the night of 23 Febr ary 1820. The scene is based on t account of Ruthven, the Bow Stre runner.

with brothels, and in reports of the fraud and knavery practised on the unsuspecting. Seamen, in particular, were the prey of 'crimps' and prostitutes who fastened on to them as soon as they left their ships, their pockets bulging with several months' wages. The crimps provided the seamen with food, drink and clothes at exorbitant rates, and thus got a legal hold on future earnings for the discharge of these debts. Seamen hooked in this way were supplied to outgoing vessels, the captains paying out 'crimpage money'.

Drunken sailors were among the regular customers of the more doubtful brothels, and of the disreputable parsons who officiated at Fleet marriages. Before Chancellor Hardwicke's Marriage Act of 1753 a marriage was valid even if there were no banns, licence, parson or other formality. Certain places in Southwark, the King's Bench Prison, and particularly, the 'Rules' or area around the Fleet Prison, became the centres for irregular wedding proceedings presided over by 'a squalid, profligate fellow clad in a tattered plaid night-gown, with a fiery face and ready to couple you for a dram of gin or a roll of tobacco'. Fleet marriages were convenient for those bent on seduction, bigamy, or merely a drunken frolic. Fortune-hunters trapped heirs and heiresses, and women in debt cleared themselves by marrying male debtors already insolvent; while female paupers were hitched on to some willing or unwilling partner in order to provide them with a new settlement and so take them off the poor rolls of their own churchwardens. One of the more advantageous facilities was that, for a consideration, an entry in the Fleet registers could be forged, changed or expunged. A certain clergyman named John Gaynam, otherwise Dr Gainham, officiated at the Fleet from 1709 to 1740. An anecdote tells of his giving evidence at the Old Bailey on the trial of Robert Hussey for bigamy in 1733:

*Above* A Fleet wedding, 'between a brisk young sailor and his landlady's daughter', 1747. Rival parsons compete for the chance to officiate.

*Dr Gainham*: The ninth of September 1733 I married a couple at the Rainbow Coffee House, the corner of Fleet Ditch, and entered the marriage in my register, as fair a register as any church in England can produce. I showed it last night to the foreman of the jury, and my Lord Mayor's Clerk, at the London Punch House.

*Counsel*: Are you not ashamed to come and own a clandestine marriage in the face of a court of justice?

*Dr Gainham* (bowing): *Video meliora, deteriora sequor* [I see what is good, but I follow the bad].

Other low parsons at the Fleet included a William Wyatt, who officiated from 1713 to 1750, moving his headquarters in the

147

meanwhile from the Two Sawyers at the corner of Fleet Lane to the Hand and Pen near Holborn Bridge; and a John Floud, who conducted marriages from 1709 to 1729, and was for some years himself a prisoner in the Fleet.

As London grew and attracted ever more people from the country and small towns, from the remote valleys and high-lands of Scotland or Wales, and from the Irish bogs, so there was increasing pressure on available living space. Suburbs expanded and more houses were built but, at least for the poor, supply always lagged behind demand. Some of the migrants arrived in the capital with only a pitiful bundle or just the clothes they stood in. Unless they were fortunate in finding employment right away they were obliged to join the indefinite, constantly changing army of the poor, whose only permanent home was the streets. At night the destitute might seek out the indifferent, often hostile shelter of a workhouse; often they made do with a dry place under an arch or in a protected corner of a yard; or they crept into a doorway and took refuge on a staircase. Those more fortunate, with a shilling or two gained from some temporary job, running an errand or begging, resorted to the common lodging-houses, where they might have a straw or flock bed for twopence or threepence the night. Lodging-houses were often primitive, dirty, decrepit and insanitary; great conveyors of infectious disease; and inflexibly harsh in turning out their customers at crack of dawn. Some were worked on a double shift, with nightworkers sleeping by day in the beds just vacated from the night before, and it was said 'the beds never got cold'. Many of the regular customers of lodging-houses were Irish, and the landladies were often Irish too – some of them managed to amass a considerable fortune after a few years in the business.

The continuous growth of London, the cramming of ever greater masses of humanity into expanding but limited spaces, the conversion of houses into shops, warehouses and workshops, the extension of markets, mills, breweries, factories and work-places of all kinds – all put pressure on the housing resources of the capital. Overcrowding of dwelling-houses was very common in the Georgian period. Many very poor families lived in a single room, or worse, in a cold, low-ceilinged garret or a damp, badly-lit cellar. At the end of the eighteenth century a doctor familiar with the slum areas commented that between three and eight persons of different sex and ages might sleep in a single bed, with the bedding rarely changed. Much of the space available in the room would be taken up by the tools or stock of some trade, while beyond the confines of the room itself

*Top* Distress in a garret, where this family of four live in a single room 1751.

148

*Above* A milk seller with his milkmaids, by George Scharf the Elder, 1818.

the malodorous no-man's-land of passages and staircases became repositories of filth and refuse. The ground floor of a house was often occupied by the owner or main tenant, and the remaining floors were sublet to families of varying income and social standing, depending on the situation of the rooms in the house, and whether a garret or cellar. Under such circumstances houses soon deteriorated, were ill-kept and delapidated; windows became grimed over and impossible to open; wood or paper replaced broken panes, and rags were stuffed into crevices to keep out draughts; the steps leading down to the basement or cellars became broken and dangerous; staircases were often rickety, ceilings cracked, roofs leaky and chimneys ready to fall in the first gale.

Street stalls and sheds used for trade by day served as cold, congested bunkhouses at night for many of the street-traders. Cellars with access from the street were both homes and places of business for cobblers, greengrocers and dealers in old clothes. Cellars formed a convenient base, and a place to keep the pails and tallies, for the milk-sellers who had a 'walk' in the neighbourhood. In criminal haunts some cellars served as night drinking places where thieves and fences gathered. Many cellar inhabitants were Irish labourers who brought with them the habit of sharing their dwelling with their animals: pigs, chickens, asses, and dogs. They sometimes let out their spare sleeping space as a means of livelihood, and it was said that as many as 40 people might be jammed into one dark, insanitary cellar. Irish lodgers with a room in a dwelling-house sometimes let one of their beds to a lodger, or even half a bed. Fearful overcrowding of this sort was not made more pleasant by the custom of holding wakes over the corpse of a deceased member of the family. The Irish were particularly addicted to this, and friends and relatives came in to drink and talk for several days, or until enough money had been collected to pay for the funeral. Meanwhile the family continued to live in the same room as the corpse, keeping it on the bed during the day, and moving it onto the table at night.

The small shopkeepers and artisans who occupied modest dwelling-houses made a practice of letting off rooms for additional income. Servants and apprentices bedded down in a garret or in the shop among the stock. There was always a large floating population of single wage-earners who rented a room for between 2s and 3s 6d a week, although rents increased rapidly during the Napoleonic Wars. A rung below the wage-earners were the casually employed 'who rise up every morning without knowing how they are to be supported during the passing day, or where in many instances they are to lodge on the succeeding night', composed, according to Colquhoun, of 'above twenty thousand miserable individuals'. These were the frequenters of the common lodging-houses, night cellars, ale-house yards and galleries of inns. It was in part the overcrowded and uncomfortable nature of many people's lodgings that made them regular patrons of certain inns or coffee houses, and when they were wanted it was there that people enquired for them. Accommodation had to be reasonably near the source of employment; indeed, many people literally lived on top of their job. There was no public transport that ordinary workers could afford, and only the wealthier merchants and business-men deserted the City and East End each evening for an Essex village or the country-like surroundings of London's western suburbs. However, the considerable distances which some people had to go to work are surprising, and walking was evidently not considered the hardship that it is today.

With the spread of the built-up area and the overcrowding of so many houses, and with the growth, too, of street-trading, shops, breweries, mills, warehouses and industrial establish-ments of all kinds, great pressure was put on London's resources of water-supply and sanitation. London's rivers had long been tapped for water for domestic as well as industrial purposes. As far back as the reign of James I (1603–25) the New River Company had provided the first organized water-supply, bringing its water by aqueduct 38 miles from springs in Hert-fordshire and from the River Lea as far as the King's Cross Road, and distributing it to consumers by means of wooden pipes. Numerous other companies followed suit during the eighteenth century. The Chelsea Water Company, founded in 1724, drew its water from the Thames and the Westbourne. The latter stream rose on the west side of Hampstead and flowed through Kilburn into Hyde Park, crossed Knightsbridge, and joined the Thames by Chelsea Hospital. In 1730 its valley through Hyde Park was dammed to form the Serpentine. The Chelsea Company used a Newcomen atmospheric steam-engine to pump its water to a reservoir on the site of Victoria Station, whence it was distributed in wooden pipes. These be-gan to be replaced by iron pipes in the 1750s, but it was not until 1829 that James Simpson, the Company's engineer, introduced an efficient sand-filter treatment to purify the water. The South London Waterworks, established in 1805, drew its water from the Thames and Vauxhall Creek: the famous Oval gasholder stands on the site of its reservoirs.

Among London's other small rivers used for domestic water

A view of the Chelsea waterworks, 1752. Notice the massive beam engine used for pumping, and the crude pipes on the ground nearby.

150

was the Wandle, which flowed from Carshalton through Mitcham to Wandsworth, and so to the Thames. Wandsworth was then a harbour of some importance, and the famous Iron Railway of 1801 was originally intended to run from Wandsworth as far as Portsmouth, though it never got further than Merstham. The Wandle flowed at the bottom of Lady Hamilton's garden, and Nelson liked to fish in it. One difficulty arising from using these rivers as a water supply was that a number, where they flowed through private grounds, were dammed up to form ornamental lakes. This was the case with the Effra and the Brent, and the Tyburn was used to form the Welsh Harp in Regent's Park. More serious as regards water-supply was the growth of mills and various noxious trades on the river banks. The Lea and the Ravensbourne (which flowed from Bromley north to Deptford Creek), were much used by mills. Dyeworks, paper mills, breweries, tanneries and many other establishments drew on the water and poured their waste materials into the streams, making them increasingly unfit for human use. The Fleet, which rose on Hampstead Heath, followed a course down to Camden Town, past old St Pancras Church, and along the line of Farringdon Street to the Thames. In 1577 a tributary of the Fleet had been used by William Lambe as a source for his conduit. The lower part of the Fleet, where it entered the Thames, was used for shipping and wharves, but became such an obstacle to east-west street traffic that it was partly covered over. Its use as a sewer and its contamination by rubbish caused such offence that towards the middle of the eighteenth century it was finally covered over completely. Before this Pope had commemorated its turgid, black flood in 'Dunciad', Book II:

> *Fleet-Ditch with desemboguing streams,*
> *Rolls the large tribute of dead dogs to Thames,*
> *The King of Dykes! than whom no sluice of mud*
> *With deeper sable blots the silver flood.*

In the crowded east and south of London the water supply was far less adequate than in the superior residential districts of the west. In the area served by the Southwark Company, for instance, some 30,000 persons had no supply at all. Even in 1850 it was estimated that 80,000 houses in London, inhabited by over 600,000 people, were still not supplied with water. At Jacob's Island, Bermondsey, it was possible to see 'at any time of day women dipping water, with pails attached by ropes to the backs of the houses, from a foul foetid ditch, its banks coated with a compound of mud and filth, and with

athing in the Fleet River, 1740. lthough the river was filled with ubbish and sewage, it was still used by he poor for bathing, and even as a ource of drinking water.

151

offal and carrion – the water to be used for every purpose, culinary ones not excepted'.

Many families relied on shallow wells, whose water filtered through neighbouring yards filled with refuse, or drained through nearby burial grounds. Otherwise they used the water companies' public fountains and standpipes, which, however, provided only an intermittent supply, available at certain hours. Residents had therefore to fetch the water when it was turned on at the standpipe, and store it in some receptacle – buckets, tubs, even soup plates were used. The limited supply meant that water was used sparingly, often two or three times over. Worst of all, the main source of most of the company water, the 'silver flood' of the Thames, was increasingly polluted by the proliferation of docks, shipping and the multitude of works along its banks, as well as by the sewers which poured their contribution of rain-diluted sewage into the main stream. The Grand Junction Company pumped its water from a point opposite the Ranelagh sewer, and filtering of domestic water supplies was not the rule until the second half of the nineteenth century. On hot summer days the stench from the Thames was unpleasant, to say the least, and at one time it was even suggested that the Houses of Parliament should move to a more salubrious site. The water companies admitted that the dilute sewage which they supplied was 'not so pleasant' to the taste, and left a sediment in the glass; but fortunately, they believed, the bulk of the consumers preferred something stronger.

If water-supplies were defective, drainage and sanitation were even worse. Early in the Georgian period the streets were widely used as receptacles for the refuse of houses and workshops. The kennel, or gutter in the centre of the street, was designed to carry away the surface water, but was often choked with mud, horse dung and dead dogs. It was not so many years earlier that an order had prohibited 'urine or ordure' from being cast into the street before nine at night, the order specifying that in fact it was not to be cast out from the houses but brought down and laid in the gutter. The new Georgian houses in the elegant streets and squares of the West End were built with brick drains leading to a public sewer below the road, or if there was no sewer to a cesspool in the garden. A privy or 'bog-house' was provided at the back of the house or in the garden, and the brick-lined circular pit below was connected to the main drain. A cistern of water was sometimes provided for flushing the pit, but the automatic water closet, fitted with a trap, did not begin to come in until the

*Above* The inadequacy of the water supply in the poor districts of London persisted long into the Victorian era, as is shown by this illustration of conditions in Bethnal Green in 1863.

*Right* A rather grandiose advertisement by a Southwark nightman (1788).

end of the eighteenth century.

The first patent for a water-closet was taken out by Alexander Cummings in 1775, and Joseph Bramah's valve-closet followed three years later. The subsequent introduction of the water-closet into the better houses proceeded only gradually, but served to emphasize the unsuitable condition of the public sewers to which they were connected. These were built of brick, flat-bottomed and flat-sided, and tended to clog up with deposits. Offensive odours penetrated fashionable streets from manholes and gratings, and sewer men were employed to go down and clear the blockages. Finally the sickening stream of sewage slopped out of the sewers directly into the Thames, to be stirred up by the tide and combined with all the refuse of the shipping and the outpourings of industrial waste matter; and the resulting mixture was then pumped up and supplied as drinking water to the richest city in the world.

Sanitation in the East End, like the water-supply, was even worse than in the residential areas of the west. Midden privies and cesspools, infrequently emptied by the night-soil men, were in common use. Houses were inadequately provided with drains, and cellars sometimes directly adjoined a midden or cesspool. This combined with the paving over of small streams and rivers made houses damp and unhealthy, and helped give rise to a complaint known as the 'London ague'. Many of the poor had no regular access to a privy, and alleys and backyards stank of urine and human excrement. To this was added the refuse of the various trades of the district, the offal of the slaughterhouses, ashes, horse dung, sweepings of stables and streets, rotting vegetables and food leavings. Night-soil contractors might remove the rubbish to their yards, but there it was allowed to rot down and mellow, causing plagues of flies in the summer months. Eventually it was carted out or sent by barge to the farmers and market gardeners as town manure. As late as the 1850s the small farmers of the Surrey clays claimed that it was impossible for them to cultivate their land without liberal dressings of the 'London muck'.

But as London grew the supply of night-soil, ashes and refuse outstripped demand. Cartage from the older, more central districts absorbed all the profit, and it remained uncollected. The average charge of £1 for emptying cesspools deterred the poorer householders from having the work done at all regularly. Privies overflowed into yards and basements. Old cesspool walls cracked and leaked their contents into the surrounding soil, and sewage oozed into nearby cellars and contaminated wells. But the picture was not entirely one of unrelieved filth and

153

squalor. Even in the districts inhabited by the very poor some streets were much better than others. A great deal depended on the character and employment of the inhabitants, the standards set by the best families, and the efforts of the local authorities. There were some well-known black spots, whose names crop up over and over again in connection with over-crowding, insanitary conditions and outbreaks of disease. Among these, said Dr Willar, writing in 1801, were 'some streets in St Giles parish, the courts and alleys adjoining to Liquor Pond Street, Hog Island, Turnmill Street, Old Street, White-cross Street, Grub Street, Golden Lane, the two Brook Lanes, Rosemary Lane, Petticoat Lane, Lower East Smithfield, some parts of Upper Westminster, and several streets of Rotherhithe etc . . .'

One of London's worst sanitary problems was the over-crowding of the graveyards. Though the city's population grew continuously, the space available for new graves was limited. The two churchyards of St Andrew's Holborn, less than an acre combined, were 'so offensive' in 1720 that they were shut up. However, they continued in use until 1747 when the parish, faced with a doubling of the population, was forced to buy up more land for burials. The 'poor's holes' were also a scandal. Large holes were opened in the graveyards for those whose relations could not afford a better grave, and they were kept open till filled up. The pits were large enough to take three or four coffins abreast and about seven in depth, and as one pit was filled, another was opened at the side of it. Complaints were made about these pits in St Martin's, St James's and St Giles in the Fields, as well as other graveyards: 'how noisome the stench is that arises from these holes so stowed with dead bodies, especially in sultry seasons and after rain, one may appeal to all who approach them . . .' The practice of making poor's holes was still prevalent, apparently, at the end of the century.

The cleaning of the streets in east London was mainly carried out to facilitate the movement of traffic, and beyond that the authorities, alarmed by the great expense of cartage, were not willing to do more. In some areas the filthy conditions of streets and courts could be traced to the neglect of regulations, and the complicated division of responsibilities between separate and sometimes overlapping authorities. Among the nuisances of the earlier Georgian period were the lack of street lighting over large parts of the capital, the prevalence of broken pavements, openings to cellars and coal-holes left dangerously uncovered, and streets choked with stalls and

Will: Conaway
near the Bull head in Dean-street
By St Anns Church.
Furnisheth Persons of Quality & others
with Lamps, Lanthorns & Irons of all sorts
Also keeps Servants to Light then
at Reasonable rates.

154

sheds. Reaction to the capital's problems was slow at first, but after about 1750 there was a growing appreciation of the need for action; despite the conditions just described, a great deal in fact was done to improve London in the Georgian era.

Before this the Great Fire of 1666 had cleared away a large area of the oldest part of the city, and of the 13,000 houses destroyed by the Fire only 9,000 were subsequently rebuilt. Brick houses replaced the old half-timbered and lath-and-plaster structures. Permanent street lighting, as distinct from the old system of providing lights only in winter (and then only up to midnight), began to appear in some areas of the capital from 1736. The Thames was embanked from London Bridge to the Fleet, and the 'stinking Fleet' itself was in stages covered over. New roads were built on both sides of the river when Westminster and Blackfriars bridges were completed in the 1750s. On the north side of town the New Road opened the way to expansion in and beyond Marylebone and Islington, and the widening of existing roads in the City was gradually undertaken after 1760. Many of these developments not only provided new amenities but also involved the clearing away of decayed, overcrowded areas of tumble-down buildings.

Progress in the reign of George III (1760–1820) depended heavily on bodies known as improvement commissions. These commissions were appointed under private Acts obtained by the various London parishes for the purpose of providing specific services: paving, street lighting, drainage, cleansing and removal of obstructions. Such Acts had already been foreshadowed by the private legislation which allowed the inhabitants of London's fashionable squares to enclose their open grounds, plant them, and protect them from damage and the dumping of rubbish. The great starting point of the improvement commissions was the Westminster Paving Act of 1762. This, the forerunner of many similar Acts, replaced the individual householder's responsibility for the paving in front of his own house by giving authority to a permanent body of commissioners, who employed staff to ensure that the work was carried out, and that damage and nuisances were prevented. As the result of the efforts of the commissions, stone replaced pebble surfaces, pavements were properly flagged, and the old central kennel gave way to gutters on each side of the street. Fire plugs were provided, and more adequate drains built. Henceforth pedestrians were less likely to fall down open coal chutes, run their heads against oversized shop signs, or be dowsed by rainwater spouting across the pavement from rooftop gutters.

As an indication of what was achieved by these commissions, not many years had passed before enthusiastic foreign visitors were extolling London's finely-paved and well-lit thoroughfares. According to Archenholtz, when the Prince of Monaco came to London at the invitation of George III he arrived in the evening and mistook the brilliant lighting of the streets as special illuminations done in his honour. Indeed, in view of the controversies which raged round the capital's deficiencies in the middle of the nineteenth century, it is important to notice that in respect of housing, water-supply, drainage, paving, lighting and general cleanliness, London was well in advance of other European cities. This situation was entirely due to the work of the enlightened parish authorities and improvement commissions in the late Georgian period. However, certain very poor areas, the slums of St Giles, Holborn, Whitechapel and Southwark, in particular, had been bypassed by the general march of progress. It was these areas that attracted the special notice of sanitary reformers during the period of the great cholera epidemics in the middle of the nineteenth century. By then, too, the improvement commissions, with their parochial boundaries, and their restricted and sometimes overlapping jurisdictions, were seen by the new, radical enthusiasts for governmental reform as obsolete, inefficient and obscurantist, though they had served the capital well enough in their day. Their weakness was that they relied on parochial pride and local means of revenue to stimulate public improvement, while in the areas of the worst slums and rookeries, with their poverty-stricken and partially transient populations, these resources were not to be found.

As such areas festered and decayed, progress continued in the better parts of London. Water-supplies improved from the 1750s with the use of iron pipes and the establishment of further water companies, though both the quality of the water and the intermittent nature of the supply left still a great deal to be desired. Street lighting, admired as it had been in the eighteenth century, was totally revolutionized by the introduction of gas lamps from 1807: by the 1830s well over 200 miles of London streets in the main residential and commercial districts were lit by gas. Medical advances, and the more enlightened treatment adopted in hospitals and dispensaries, reduced the toll exacted by the great killing diseases. In the later eighteenth century inoculation, and subsequently vaccination introduced by Jenner in 1796, reduced and eventually ended the ravages of smallpox. Typhus, the plague of poverty, a regular visitor of the prisons, workhouses and hospitals,

The rookeries of Victorian London, the seed-beds of cholera, had their origin in the untended slums of the Georgian era.

faded with the isolation of the stricken and the cleansing of infected houses. Deaths from typhus fell by over two-thirds, from an average of 3,188 a year in the eighteenth century to only 1,033 in 1815.

In some regards such as housing and street improvement, the long period of warfare between 1793 and 1815 was responsible for slowing down the rate of progress. In the war years interest rates were high, money was short, taxes increased and the imported timber used for house-building became scarce and expensive. A big expansion of housing, and of water- and gas-supplies, followed in the cheaper post-war period, though some projects, such as the London docks, the Foundling and Bedford estates in Bloomsbury, and the building of the new Bank of England by Sir John Soane, had managed to go ahead during the war years.

London was thus vastly improved, although Francis Place was overstating the case when he claimed in 1824 that the 'half-starved, miserable, scald-headed children with rickety limbs and bandy legs' of his youth had disappeared. It was probably true, however, that the majority of people were 'better dressed, better fed, cleaner, better educated' than he remembered them to have been a few decades before. They were also, he thought, better housed. Visiting Walworth in 1832, Place remarked on the varied condition of the houses occupied by the poor. Some, he said, were 'in a very bad state'. But the streets 'are none of them narrow . . . Some of them are of considerable width – as much I think as thirty feet, and one or two, the houses in which are only one or two stories high, must be forty feet wide. Many of these streets are inhabited by very poor people – but neither the streets nor the houses are by any means so dirty as were the narrow streets and lanes which have been destroyed to make way for modern improvements – nor do they stink as such places used to do.' Even old areas, like the streets in Lambeth occupied by poor Thames fishermen, and still paved with pebbles, were now clean and well-kept, and the inhabitants themselves were also much cleaner:

> Formerly the women young and old were seen emptying their pails or pans at the doors, or washing on stools in the street, in the summer time without gowns on their backs or handkerchiefs on their necks, their leather stays half laced and as black as the door posts, their black coarse worsted stockings and striped linsey-wolsey petticoats 'standing alone with dirt'. No such things are seen now. Compared with themselves at the two periods, even these peoples are gentlefolks. (Quoted by Dorothy George in *London Life in the Eighteenth Century*)

157

Against the improvements noticed by Place have to be set the continued filth and squalor of the slums, the disgusting conditions of the prisons and workhouses, and the scandal of the criminal rookeries. These were the continuing blights against which Dickens and the Victorian sanitary reformers, Chadwick and Simon, campaigned. As old rookeries were pulled down, and as docks, warehouses, new bridges and other developments made inroads into the housing available to the poor, so the displaced inhabitants moved on to create greater overcrowding elsewhere. The problems of housing, and of supplying London's population with the basic requirements of civilized existence, were continuing ones. 'On reading the descriptions of the state of London in the eighteen-forties', remarks Dorothy George, 'it is hard to realize that things could ever have been worse. Yet there is much evidence that they had.' Georgian London, despite all the problems left untouched, had made progress, and this notwithstanding the rapid growth of its population. It left behind a legacy of great neglect, but bequeathed also a remarkable tradition of reform which went far to ease the gradual transition to the modern metropolis.

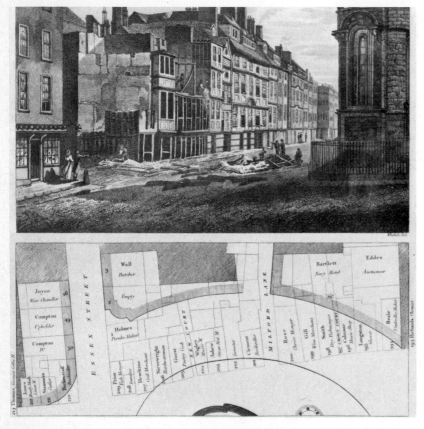

The Strand at a point of change: some of the buildings have already been demolished prior to the street's widening and improvement, 1810.

# Select Bibliography

R J Allen, *The Clubs of Augustan London* (Archon, Hamden, Conn., 1967)

C Bruyn Andrews, ed., *The Torrington Diaries* (Eyre & Spottiswoode, 1935)

W Von Archenholtz, *A View of the British Constitution and of the Manners and Customs of the People of England* (1794 ed.)

J Bagley, ed., *The Great Diurnal of Nicholas Blundell of Little Crosby, Lancashire* (Record Society of Lancashire & Cheshire, Chester, 1968–70)

R Bayne-Powell, *Eighteenth-Century London Life* (John Murray, 1937)

Gillian Bebbington, *London Street Names* (Batsford, 1972)

E W Bovill, *English Country Life 1780–1830* (OUP, 1962)

E Beresford Chancellor, *The Eighteenth Century in London* (Batsford, 1920)

Daniel Defoe, *A Tour through England and Wales* (Everyman ed., 1928)

G Eland, ed., *Purefoy Letters 1735–53* (Sidgwick & Jackson, 1931)

F J Fisher, 'The Development of London as a Centre of Conspicuous Consumption in the Sixteenth and Seventeenth Centuries', *Transactions of the Royal Historical Society* (1948)

Denys Forrest, *Tea for the British* (Chatto & Windus, 1973)

G E and K R Fussell, *The English Countrywoman A.D. 1500–1900* (A Melrose, 1953)

Dorothy George, 'London and the Life of the Town', in A S Turberville, ed., *Johnson's England* (OUP, 1933)

Dorothy George, *London Life in the Eighteenth Century* (Kegan Paul, 1930)

John H Harvey, 'The Stocks held by early Nurseries', *Agricultural History Review* XXII, 1 (1974)

A P Herbert, *Mr Guy's London* (1948)

A E J Hollaender and W Kellaway, *Studies in London History* (Hodder & Stoughton, 1969)

W H Irving, *John Gay's London* (Archon, Cambridge, Mass., 1928)

Henry Jephson, *The Sanitary Evolution of London* (Blom, New York, 1907)

David J Johnson, *Southwark and the City* (OUP, 1969)

R A Lewis, *Edwin Chadwick and the Public Health Movement 1832–54* (Longmans, 1952)

W S Lewis, *Three Tours through London in the Years 1748, 1776, 1797* (Yale University Press, New Haven, Conn., 1941)

Robert W Malcolmson, *Popular Recreations in English Society 1700–1850* (CUP, 1973)

Dorothy Marshall, *Dr Johnson's London* (John Wiley, 1968)

W E Minchinton, *The Growth of English Overseas Trade in the Seventeenth and Eighteenth Centuries* (Methuen, 1969)

Donald J Olsen, *Town Planning in London: the Eighteenth and Nineteenth*

*Centuries* (Yale University Press, New Haven, Conn., 1964)

Alfred Plummer, *The London Weavers' Company 1600–1790* (Routledge & Kegan Paul, 1972)

F A Pottle, ed., *Boswell's London Journal 1762–63* (Heinemann, 1950

Steen Eiler Rasmussen, *London: the Unique City* (revised English ed. Cape, 1937)

George Rudé, *Hanoverian London 1714–1808* (Secker & Warburg 1971)

Francis Sheppard, *London 1808–70: the Infernal Wen* (Secker & Warburg, 1971)

Sir John Summerson, *Georgian London* (Pleaides Books, 1945)

Barry Supple, *The Royal Exchange Assurance* (CUP, 1970)

Ann Saunders, *Regent's Park: a Study of the Area from 1086 to the Presen Day* (Kelley, 1969)

E P Thompson, *The Making of the English Working Class* (Gollancz 1963)

A S Turberville, ed., *Johnson's England* (OUP, 1933)

J Steven Watson, *The Reign of George III 1760–1815* (OUP, 1960)

R J White, *The Age of George III* (Heinemann, 1968)

Basil Williams, *The Whig Supremacy 1714–60* (OUP, 1939)

E A Wrigley, 'A Simple Model of London's Importance in changing English Society and Economy 1650–1750', *Past & Present* 37 (1967

Arthur Young, *A Six Weeks Tour through the Southern Counties o England and Wales* (1768, reprinted Arthur J Cassell, Sittingbourne Kent, 1975)

Arthur Young *A Six Months Tour through the North of England* (1770

A game of Four Corners, played at the Swan Inn, Chelsea, *c.* 1750.

160

# Index